9/22/75

Selections from the

World's Devotional Classics

Volume VII

Marshall to Norris

Vol. Seven

John Bunyan

Selections from the World's Devotional Classics

EDITED BY

Robert Scott and George W. Gilmore

Editors of The Homiletic Review

IN TEN VOLUMES

Volume VII

Marshall to Norris

FUNK & WAGNALLS COMPANY

NEW YORK AND LONDON

Contents Volume Seven

Selections

Prayers

SELECTIONS FROM

The Gospel Mystery of Sanctification

BY

WALTER MARSHALL

WALTER MARSHALL

Presbyterian divine, born at Bishop Wearmouth, Durham, June 15, 1628. He was educated at Winchester College, then at New College, Oxford, where he graduated and was elected a fellow in the year 1650. He was presented to the living of Hursley in 1661. By the Act of Uniformity in 1662 he was ejected, but soon after that time he settled as minister of an independent congregation at Gosport, where he died in 1680. He is best known by his chief work, "The Gospel Mystery of Sanctification," of which numerous editions have been brought out.

Endeavor Diligently to Perform the Great Work of Believing On Christ, In a Right Manner, Without Any Delay, and Then Also to Continue and Increase In Your Most Holy Faith: That So Your Enjoyment of Him, Union and Fellowship With Him, and All Holiness By Him, May Be Begun, Continued, and Increased In You

Faith in Christ is the duty with which a holy life is to begin, and by which the foundation of all other holy duties is laid in the soul. It is before sufficiently proved[1] that Christ himself, with all endowments necessary to enable us to an holy practise, is received actually into our hearts by faith. This is the uniting grace, whereby the Spirit of God knitteth the knot of mystical marriage between Christ and us, and maketh us branches of that noble vine; members of that body,

[1] Preceding parts of the work deal with Christian duty under the law, the endowments and qualifications necessary to perform them, which are gained through union with Christ and fellowship with him, through faith and the gospel. Sanctification comes after union, justification, and the gift of the Holy Spirit. The comforts of the gospel enable performance of duty under law, and assurance of faith is also a necessity.

joined to that excellent head; living stones of that spiritual temple, built upon the precious living corner-stone and sure foundation; partakers of the bread and drink that came down from heaven and giveth life to the world. This is the grace whereby we pass from our corrupt natural state to a new holy state in Christ, also from death in sin to the life of righteousness; and whereby we are comforted, that so we may be established in every good word and work. If we put the question, "What must we do that we may work the works of God?" Christ resolveth it, that we "believe on him whom he hath sent" (John 6:28, 29). He putteth us first upon the work of believing, which is the work by God, by way of eminency, the work of works, because all other good works proceed from it.

The first thing in the present direction, is to put you upon the performance of this great work of believing on Christ, and to guide you therein, for you are to consider distinctly four things contained in it.

1. The first is, you are to make it your diligent endeavor to perform the great work of believing on Christ. Many make little conscience of this duty. It is not known by natural light, as many moral duties are, but only by supernatural revelation in the gospel, and it is foolishness to the natural man.

These are sometimes terrified with apprehensions of other sins, and will examine themselves concerning them and, it may be, will write them down to help their memories and devotion. But the great sin of not believing on Christ is seldom thought of in their self-examinations or registered in the large catalogs of their sins. And even those who are convinced that believing on Christ is a duty necessary to salvation, do neglect all diligent endeavors to perform it; either because they account that it is a motion of the heart which may be easily performed at any time, without any labor or diligent endeavors; or, on the contrary, because they account it as difficult as all the works of the law, and utterly impossible for them to perform by their most diligent endeavors, except the Spirit of God work it in them by his mighty power; and that therefore it is in vain for them to work, until they feel this working of the Spirit in their hearts: or because they account it a duty so peculiar to the elect that it would be presumption for them to endeavor the performance of it until they know themselves to be elected to eternal life through Christ. I shall urge you to diligent performance of this duty, notwithstanding all these impediments, by the following consideration. It is worthy of our best endeavors, as appeareth by the preciousness, excellency, and necessity of it already discovered.

If the light of nature were not darkened in the matters of salvation, it would show us that we can not of ourselves find out the way of salvation, and would condemn those that despise that revelation of the way of salvation that God hath given us in the gospel, declared in the Holy Scriptures. The great end of preaching the gospel is for the obedience of faith (Rom 1:5), that so we may be brought to Christ and all other obedience. Yea, the great end of all revealed doctrines in the whole Scripture is, to "make us wise unto salvation by faith that is in Christ Jesus" (2 Tim. 3:15). The "end of the law given by Moses was for righteousness to every one that believeth" (Rom. 10:4), and Christ was that end for righteousness. The moral law itself was revealed in order to our salvation by believing on Christ; or else the knowledge of it had nothing availed fallen man, that was unable to perform it. Therefore they that slight the duty of believing, and account it foolishness, do thereby slight, despise, and vilify the whole counsel of God revealed in the Scripture. The law and the gospel and Christ himself are become of none effect to the salvation of such. The only fruit that such an one can attain to by all the saving doctrines of the Scripture is only some hypocritical moral duties and slavish performances, which will be as filthy rags in the sight of God in the great day. However, many mind not the sin of unbelief in their self-examinations, and write it not in their scrolls: yet let them know that this is the most pernicious sin of all. All the sins in their scrolls would not prevail to their condemnation; yea, they would not prevail in their conversation, were it not for their unbelief. This one sin prevailing maketh it impossible for them to please God in any duty whatsoever (Heb. 11:6). If you will not mind this one main sin now, God will at last mind you of it with a vengeance: for "he that believeth not on the Son, shall not see life: but the wrath of God abideth on him" (John 3:36). The Lord Jesus shall be revealed from heaven in flaming fire, taking vengeance on those that obey not the gospel of our Lord Jesus Christ (2. Thess. 1:7, 8).

2. Believing on Christ is a work that will require diligent endeavor and labor for the performance of it. We must labor to enter into that rest, lest any man fall by unbelief (Heb. 4:11). "We must show diligence to the full assurance of hope to the end, that we may be followers of them who through faith and patience inherit the promises" (Heb.

6:11, 12). It is a work that requireth the exercise of might and power; and therefore we have need to be strengthened with might by the spirit in the inward man, that Christ may dwell in our hearts by faith (Eph. 3:16, 17). I confess, it is easy, pleasant, and delicious in its own nature, because it is a motion of the heart, without any cumbersome bodily labor: and it is a taking Christ and his salvation as our own, which is very comfortable and delightful; and the soul is carried forth in this, by love to him and its own happiness, which is an affection that maketh even hard works easy and pleasant; yet it is made difficult to us, by reason of the opposition that it meets with from our own inward corruptions and from Satan's temptations. It is no easy matter to receive Christ as our happiness and free salvation, with true confidence and lively affection, when the guilt of sin lieth heavily upon the conscience, and the wrath of God is manifested by the word and terrible judgments: especially when we have been long accustomed to seek salvation by the procurement of our own works, and to account the way of salvation by free grace foolish and pernicious; when our lusts incline us strongly to the things of the flesh and the world; when Satan doth his utmost, by his own suggestions, and by false teachers, and by worldly allurements and terrors, to hinder the sincere performance of this duty. Many works that are easy in their own nature prove difficult for us to perform in our circumstances. To forgive our enemies and to love them as ourselves is but a motion of the mind, easy to be performed in its own nature; and yet many that are convinced of their duty find it a hard matter to bring their hearts to the performance of it. It is but a motion of the mind to cast our care upon God for worldly things, and rich men may think they can do it easily; but poor men, that have great families, find it a hard matter. That easy comfortable duty which Moses exhorted the Israelites to, when Pharaoh with his chariots and horsemen overtook them at the Red Sea, "Fear ye not, stand still, and see the salvation of the Lord, which he will show to you to-day" (Ex. 14:13), was not easily performed. The very easiness of some duties make their performance difficult; as Naaman the Syrian was hardly brought to wash and be clean, because he thought it to be too slight and easy a remedy for the cure of his leprosy (2 Kings 5:12, 13). Even in this very case people are offended at the duty of believing on Christ as too light and easy a remedy to cure the leprosy of the soul; they would have some harder thing enjoined them to the attainment of so great an end as this everlasting salvation. The performance of all the moral law is not accounted work enough for this end (Matt. 19:17, 20). However easy the work of believing seemeth to many; yet common experience hath showed that men are more easily brought to the most burdensome, unreasonable, and inhuman observations; as the Jews and Christian Galatians were more easily brought to take upon their necks the yoke of Moses' law, which none were able to bear (Acts 15:10). The heathens were more easily brought to burn their sons and daughters in the fire to their gods (Deut. 12:31). . . . They that slight the work of faith for its easiness show that they were never yet made sensible of innumerable sins and of the terrible curse of the law and wrath of God that they lie under; and of the darkness and vanity of their minds, the corruption and hardness of their hearts, and their bondage under the power of sin and Satan; and have not been truly humbled, without which they can not believe in a right manner. Many sound believers have found by experience that it hath been a very hard matter to bring their hearts to the duty of believing; it hath cost them vigorous struggles and sharp conflicts with their own corruptions and Satan's temptations. It is so difficult a work that we can not perform it without the mighty working of the Spirit of God in our hearts, who only can make it to be absolutely easy to us, and doth make it easy or suffer it to be difficult, according as he is pleased to communicate his grace in various degrees unto our souls.

3. Tho we can not possibly perform this great work in a right manner until the Spirit of God work faith in our hearts by his mighty power, yet it is necessary that we should endeavor it; and that before we can find the Spirit of God working faith effectually in us, or giving strength to believe. We can perform no holy duty acceptably, except the Spirit of God work it in us; and yet we are not hereby excused from working ourselves, but we are the rather stirred up to the greater diligence: "Work out your salvation, with fear and trembling; for it is God that worketh in you both to will and to do of his good pleasure" (Phil. 2:12, 13). The way by which the Spirit works faith in the elect is by stirring them up to endeavor to believe. And this is a way suitable to the means that the Spirit useth; *i.e.*, the exhortations, commands, and invitations of the gospel; which would be of no force, if we were not to obey them until we find faith already wrought in us. Neither can we possibly find that the Spirit of God doth effectually work faith, or

give strength to believe, until we act it; for all inward graces, as well as all other inward habits, are discerned by their acts, as seed in the ground by its springing. We can not see any such thing as love to God or man in our hearts before we act it. Children know not their ability to stand upon their feet until they have made trial by endeavoring so to do; so we know not our spiritual strength until we have learned by experience from the use and exercise of it. Neither can we know, or assure ourselves absolutely, that the Spirit of God will give us strength to believe before we act faith; for such a knowledge and assurance, if it be right, is saving faith itself in part; and whosoever trusteth on Christ assuredly for strength to believe by his Spirit doth, in effect, trust on him for his own salvation, which is inseparably joined with the grace of saving faith. Tho the Spirit worketh other duties in us by faith, yet he worketh faith in us immediately by hearing, knowing, and understanding the word: "Faith cometh by hearing, and hearing by the word of God" (Rom. 10:17). And in the word he maketh no absolute promise or declaration that he will work faith in this or that unbelieving heart, or that he will give strength to any one in particular to believe, or begin the work of believing in Christ; for faith itself is the first grace whereby we have a particular interest in any saving promise. It is a thing hidden in the secret council and purpose of God concerning us, whether he will give us his Spirit and saving faith until our election be discovered by our believing actually. Therefore, as soon as we know the duty of believing, we are to apply ourselves immediately to the vigorous performance of the duty, and in so doing we shall find that the Spirit of Christ hath strengthened us to believe, tho we know not certainly that he will do it beforehand. The Spirit cometh indiscernibly upon the elect, to work faith within them; like the wind that bloweth where it lists, and none knoweth whence it cometh, and whither it goeth, but only we hear the sound of it, and thereby know it when it is past and gone (John 3:8). We must therefore begin all the work, before we know that the Spirit doth or will work in us savingly; and we shall be willing to set upon the work, if we be Christ's people; for "thy people shall be willing in the day of thy power" (Ps. 110:3). It is enough that God discovereth to us beforehand in the gospel what faith is, and the ground we have to believe on Christ for our own salvation; and that God requireth this duty of us, and will help us in the performance of it if we apply ourselves heartily thereunto: "Fear not, I command thee, be strong and of good courage'' (Josh. 1:6); "Arise and be doing, and the Lord will be with thee'' (1. Chron. 22:16). Therefore whoso receiveth this gospel discovery as the word of God in hearty love is taught by the Spirit, and will certainly come to Christ by believing (John 6:45). Everyone that receiveth it not despiseth God, maketh him a liar, and deserveth justly to perish for his unbelief.

4. Tho the Spirit worketh saving faith only in the elect, and others believe not because they are not of Christ's sheep (John 10:26), and on that account it is called the "faith of God's elect'' (Tit. 1:1), yet all who hear the gospel are obliged to the duty of believing, as well as to all the duties of the moral law, and that before they know their own particular election; and they are liable to condemnation for unbelief as well as for any other sin: "He that believeth not, is condemned already, because he hath not believed on the name of the only begotten Son of God'' (John 3:18). The Apostle Paul showeth that the elect Israelites obtained salvation, and the rest, who were not elected, were blinded; and yet even those were broken off from the good olive-tree because of their unbelief (Rom. 11:7, 20). We can not have a certain knowledge of our election to eternal

life before we do believe; it is a thing hidden in the unsearchable council of God, until it be manifest by our effectual calling and believing on Christ. The apostle knew the election of the Thessalonians by finding the evidence of their faith that the gospel came to them, not in "word only, but also in power, and in the Holy Ghost, and in much assurance: and that they had received the word in much affliction, with joy in the Holy Ghost" (1 Thess. 1:4, 5, 6). We are to see our calling, if we would find out that God hath chosen us (1 Cor. 1:26, 27). Therefore we must believe on Christ before we know our election, or else we shall never know it and shall never believe. And it is no presumption for us to trust confidently on Christ for everlasting life before we have any good evidence of our election; because God, who can not lie, hath made a general promise, that whosoever "believeth on him shall not be ashamed," without making the least difference among them who perform this duty (Rom. 10:11, 12). The promise is as firm and sure to be fulfilled as any of God's decrees and purposes; and therefore it is a good and sufficient ground for our confidence. It is certain that all that the Father hath given to Christ by the decrees of eternal election shall come to Christ; and it is as really certain that Christ will in nowise cast out any that cometh to him, whosoever he be (John 6:37). And we need not fear that we shall infringe God's decree of election by believing on Christ confidently for our salvation, before we know what God hath decreed concerning us; for if we believe, we shall at last be found among the number of the elect; and if we refuse to believe, we shall thereby wilfully place ourselves among the reprobates, that stumble at the word, being disobedient, "whereunto also they are appointed" (1 Pet. 2:8).

I shall add further, that tho we have no evidence of our particular election before we believe, yet we are to trust on Christ assuredly to make it evident to us, by giving us that salvation which is the peculiar portion of the elect only. All spiritual saving blessings wherewith God blesseth his people in Christ are the peculiar portion of them whom "God hath chosen in Christ before the foundation of the world" (Eph. 1:3, 4), yet we must necessarily trust on Christ for those saving blessings or have none at all. We are to pray in faith, nothing doubting that God will remember us with the favor that he beareth to his people; that we may see the good of his chosen, and glory with his inheritance (Ps. 106:4, 5). Therefore we are to trust assuredly on God that he will deal with us as his chosen people. Thus it appeareth that it is not presumption, but your bounden duty, to apply yourselves to the great work of believing on Christ for salvation, without questioning at all beforehand whether you are elected or not: "secret things belong to God, but those things that are revealed, belong unto us, that we may do them" (Deut. 39:29).

The second thing directed to is that you shall endeavor for a right manner of performing this duty. This is a point of great concernment, because the want of it will render your faith ineffectual to sanctification and salvation. The great duty of love, which is the end of the law and the principal fruit of sanctification, must flow from faith unfeigned (1 Tim. 1:5). There is a feigned faith, that doth not really receive Christ into the heart, and will not produce love or any true obedience—such as Simon Magus had (Acts 8:13, 23), for, notwithstanding his faith, he was in the "gall of bitterness and in the bond of iniquity"; and such as those Jews had to whom Christ would not commit himself, who did not confess him, lest they should on that account be put out of the synagog (John 2:23; 12:43), and such as the Apostle James speaks of, "What doth it profit, my brethren, if a man say he hath faith, and have not works? Can that faith save him? The devils also believe and tremble'' (James 2:14, 19). Take heed, therefore, lest you deceive your souls with a counterfeit faith, instead of the precious faith of God's elect. The way to distinguish the one from the other is by considering well what is the right manner of that believing which is effectual to salvation. Hypocrites may perform the same works for the matter, with true saints; but they are defective in the manner of performance, wherein the excellency of the work doth chiefly consist. One great reason why many seek to enter in at the strait gate and are not able (Luke 13:24) is because they are ignorant and defective in the right manner of acting this faith whereby they are to enter. Now, I confess that God only is able to guide us effectually in the right way of believing. And we have this great consolation, when we see our own folly and proneness to mistake our way, that if we heartily desire and endeavor to believe on Christ aright, we may confidently trust on him to guide us. God hath promised, that the wayfaring men, tho fools, shall not err in the way of holiness; and that he will teach sinners in the way: ''The meek will he guide in judgment, and the meek will he teach his way'' (Ps. 25:8, 9), and he commandeth them that lack wisdom ''to ask it of God in faith, nothing doubting'' (James 1:5, 6). But, however, we are to know that God guideth us only according to the rule of his word; and we must endeavor to learn the right way of believing out of the word, or else we are not able so much as to trust rightly on God for guidance and direction in this great work. . . . Saving faith . . . containeth two acts; the one is believing the truth of the gospel, the other is believing on Christ as revealed and freely promised to us in the gospel, for all his salvation. Now, your great endeavor must be to perform both these acts in a right manner, as I shall show concerning each of them in particular.

In the first place, you are highly concerned to endeavor for a right belief of the truth of the gospel of Christ; that so you may be well furnished, disposed, and encouraged, to believe on him, as revealed and promised in the gospel. Hereby you are to remove all discomfortable thoughts and objections of Satan and your own conscience, and to overcome all corrupt inclinations that hinder a cheerful embracing of Christ and his salvation. It is found by experience that when any fail in the second act of faith, the reason of their failing is commonly some defect in this first act. There is some false imagination or other in them, contrary to the belief of the truth of the gospel, which is a stronghold of sin and Satan that must be pulled down, before they can receive Christ into their hearts by believing on him. If they knew the name of Christ as he is discovered in the gospel, and judged aright of the truth and excellency of it, they would not fail to put their trust in him. And we are in great danger of entertaining such false imaginations and to account many truths of the gospel strange paradoxes, yea, foolish and pernicious, because of our ignorance, self-conceitedness, guilty consciences, corrupt affections, and manifold errors, wherewith our judgments are prepossest in matters of salvation; and because Satan laboreth to beguile us, as he did Eve, through his subtlety, to corrupt our minds from the simplicity of the gospel that is in Christ (2 Cor. 11:3). I shall therefore give you some particular instructions that are of the greatest moment, to prevent such defects as we are most liable to in the first act of our faith.

1. You must believe with a full persuasion that you are a child of wrath by nature, as well as others; fallen from God by the sin of the first Adam; dead in trespasses and sins; subject to the curse of the law of God, and to the power of Satan, and to insupportable misery to all eternity; and that you can not

possibly procure your reconciliation with God, or any spiritual life and strength to do any good work, by any endeavoring to get salvation according to the terms of the legal covenant; and that you can not find any way to escape out of this sinful and miserable condition by your own reason and understanding without supernatural revelation, nor to be freed from it except by that infinite power that raiseth the dead. We must not be afraid, as some are, to know our own vileness and sinfulness, neither must we be willing to think ourselves better than we are; but must be heartily desirous and glad to know the worst of our own condition; yea, when we have found out the worst that we can of ourselves, we must be willing to believe that our hearts are deceitful and desperately wicked, beyond all that we can know and find out (Jer. 17:9). This is all necessary to work in us true humiliation, self-despair, and self-loathing, that we may highly esteem and earnestly seek the salvation of Christ as the one thing necessary. It maketh us sick of sin and sensible of our need of the great Physician, and willing to be ordered, according to any of his prescriptions, whatsoever we suffer, rather than to follow our own wisdom (Matt. 9:12). It was for want of this humiliation that the scribes and Pharisees were not so forward to enter into the kingdom of heaven as the publicans and harlots (Matt. 21:31).

2. You are to believe assuredly, that there is no way to be saved without receiving all the saving benefits of Christ, his Spirit as well as his merits, sanctification as well as remission of sins by faith. It is the ruin of many souls that they trust on Christ for remission of sins without any regard to holiness; whereas these two benefits are inseparably joined in him, so that none are freed from condemnation by Christ but those that are enabled to walk holily, *i.e.*, not after the flesh, but after the Spirit (Rom. 8:1). It is also the ruin of souls to seek only remission of sins by faith in Christ, and holiness by our endeavors, according to the terms of the law; whereas we can never live to God in holiness except we be dead to the law, and live only by Christ living in us by faith. That faith which receiveth not holiness as well as remission of sins from Christ will never sanctify us; and therefore it will never bring us to heavenly glory (Heb. 12:14).

3. You are to be fully persuaded of the "all-sufficiency of Christ for the salvation of yourself and of all that believe on him; that his blood cleanseth from all sin" (1 John 1:7). Tho our sins be never so great and

horrible, and continued in never so long, yet he is able to deliver from the body of death, and mortify our corruptions be they ever so strong. We find in Scripture that abominable wicked persons have been saved by him, idolaters, adulterers, effeminate, covetous, drunkards, extortioners, etc. (1 Cor. 6:9, 10). Such as have sinned against the light of nature, as the heathen, and the light of Scripture, as the Jews; such as have denied Christ, as Peter, and persecuted and blasphemed him as Paul. Many that have fallen into great sins are ruined forever, because they do not account the grace of Christ sufficient for their pardon and sanctification: when they think they are gone and past all hope of recovery, that their sins are upon them, and they pine away in them, how shall they live? (Ezek. 33:10). This despair works secretly in many souls, without such trouble and honor, and maketh them careless of their souls and true religion. The devil fills some with horrid, filthy, blasphemous thoughts, on purpose that they think their sins too great to be forgiven; tho commonly such thoughts are the least of the sins of those that are pestered with them, and rather the devil's sin than theirs, because they are hurried into them sore against their wills; but if their hearts be somewhat polluted within them, Christ testifieth "that all manner of sin and blasphemy shall be forgiven, except blasphemy against the Holy Ghost" (Matt. 12:31). And as for those that are guilty of blasphemy against the Holy Ghost, the reason why they are never forgiven is not because of any want of sufficiency in the blood of Christ, or in the pardoning mercy of God; but because they never repent of that sin, and never seek to God for mercy through him, but continue obstinate until death; for the Scripture testifieth, that it is impossible to renew them again unto repentance (Heb. 6:5, 6). So that the merits of Christ are sufficient for all that seek to him for mercy by believing. There are others that despair of ever getting any victory over their lusts, because they have formerly made many vows and resolutions and have used many vigorous endeavors against them in vain. Such are to persuade themselves that the grace of Christ is sufficient for them when all other means have failed; as the woman that had the issue of blood, and was nothing bettered but rather grew worse by any remedies that physicians could prescribe, yet persuaded herself that, if she might but touch the clothes of Christ, she should be whole (Mark 5:25-28). Those that despair, by reason of the greatness of their guilt and corruption, do greatly dishonor and undervalue the grace of God, his infinite mercy, and the infinite merits of Christ's blood, and the power of his Spirit, and deserve to perish with Cain and Judas. Abundance of people that give up themselves to all licentiousness in this wicked generation lie under secret despair; which maketh them so desperate in swearing, blaspheming, whoring, drunkenness, and all manner of wickedness. How horrid and heinous soever our sins and corruptions have been, we should learn to account them a small matter in comparison to the grace of Christ, who is God as well as man, and offered up himself, by the Eternal Spirit, as a sacrifice of infinite value, for our salvation: and can create us anew as easily as he created the world by a word speaking.

4. You are to be fully persuaded of the truth of the general free promise, in your own particular case, that if you believe on Christ sincerely, you shall have everlasting life as well as any other in the world, without performing any condition of works to procure an interest in him; for the promise is universal. "Whosoever believeth on him shall not be ashamed" (Rom. 9:33), without any exception. And if God exclude you not, you must not exclude yourselves, but rather conclude peremptorily, that how vile, wicked,

and unworthy soever you be, yet, if you come, you shall be accepted as well as any other in the world. You are to believe that great article of the creed, the remission of sins, in your own case, when you are principally concerned, or else it will little profit you to believe it in the case of others. This is that which hinders many broken, wounded spirits from coming to the great Physician, when they are convinced of the abominable filthiness of their hearts, that they are dead in sin without the least spark of true grace and holiness in them. They think that it is in vain for such as they are to trust on Christ for salvation, and that he will never save such as they are. Why so? they can be but lost creatures at worst; and Christ came to seek and save those that are lost. If they that are dead in sin can not be saved, then all must despair and perish; for none have any spiritual life until they receive it by believing on Christ. Some think themselves to be worse than any others, and that none have such wicked hearts as they: and tho others be accepted, yet they shall be rejected. But they should know that Christ came to save the chief of sinners (1 Tim. 1:15); and that the design of God is to show the exceeding riches of his grace in our salvation (Eph. 2:7), which is most glorified by pardoning the greatest sinners.

And it is but our ignorance to think ourselves like nobody; for all others, as well as we, are naturally dead in trespasses and sins; their mind is enmity to God, and is not subject to his law, nor indeed can be (Rom. 8:7), and every imagination of the thoughts of their hearts are only evil, and continually so (Gen. 6:5); they have all the same corrupt fountain of all abominations in their hearts, tho we may have exceeded many others in several actual sins. Others think that they have outstaid their time, and therefore now they should find no place for repentance, tho they should seek it carefully with tears (Heb. 12:17). But, behold "now is the accepted time; behold, now is the day of salvation" (2 Cor. 6:2), even as God calleth upon you by the gospel. And altho Esau was rejected, who sought rather the earthly than the spiritual blessings of the birthright; yet they shall not be rejected that seek the enjoyment of Christ and his salvation as their only happiness. If you come unto Christ's vineyard at the eleventh hour of the day, you shall have your penny, as well as those that came early in the morning; because the reward is of grace, and not of merit (Matt. 10:9, 10). And here you must be sure to believe stedfastly that Christ and all his salvation is bestowed as a free gift upon those that do not work to procure any right or title to him, or meetness or unworthiness to receive him, but only believe on him that justifieth the ungodly (Rom. 4:5). If you put any condition of works or good qualifications between yourselves and Christ, it will be a partition wall which you can never climb over.

5. You are to believe assuredly that it is the will of God you should believe in Christ and have eternal life by him, as well as any other; that your believing is a duty very acceptable to God; and that he will help you, as well as any other, in this work, because he calleth and commandeth you, by the gospel, to believe on him. This maketh us to set cheerfully upon the work of believing; as when Jesus commanded the blind man to be called, they said unto him, "Be of good comfort, rise; he calleth thee" (Mark 10:49). A command of Christ made Peter to walk upon the water (Matt. 14:29). And here we are not to meddle with God's secret of predestination, or the purpose of his will to give the grace of faith to some rather than others; but only with his revealed will, in his gracious invitations and commands, by which we are required to believe on Christ. This will of God is confirmed by his oath, "As I live, saith the Lord God, I have no pleasure in the death of the wicked, but that the

wicked turn from his way, and live: turn ye, turn ye, from your evil ways; for why will ye die, O house of Israel'' (Ezek. 33:11). Christ testifieth that he ''would often have gathered the children of Jerusalem, even as a hen gathereth her chickens under her wings, and they would not'' (Matt 23:37). And the Apostle Paul testifieth that God ''will have all men to be saved'' (1 Tim. 2:4). You are to reject and abandon all thoughts that are contrary to this persuasion. What if few be saved? thy salvation will not make the number too great; for few will follow thee in the duty of believing. What if the wrath of God be revealed from heaven against thee in many terrible judgments, and the word and thine own conscience condemn thee, and Christ seem to reckon thee no better than a dog, as he did the woman of Canaan (Matt. 15:26)? Thou art to make a good interpretation of all these things, that the end of them is to drive thee to Christ, as this was the end of the curses of the law and all the terrible dispensations of them (Rom. 10:4). If a prophet or an angel from heaven were sent of God, on purpose to declare that the sentence of everlasting damnation is declared against thee, it would be thy duty to believe that God sent him to give thee timely warning for this very end, that thou mightest believe and turn to God by faith and repentance. Jeremiah prophesied against the Jews, that God would pluck them up, pull them down, and destroy them for their sins; yet he himself taught them, "if they turned from their evil ways, God would repent him of the evil" (Jer. 18:11). Jonah preached nothing but certain destruction to Nineveh to be executed upon them within forty days (chapter 3:4), yet the intent of that terrible message was that those heathenish people might escape destruction by repentance. The most absolute and peremptory denunciations of divine vengeance against us, while we are in this world, must always be understood with a secret reserve of salvation for us, upon our faith and repentance. And we are to account that the reason why God doth so terribly denounce his judgments against us by his word is that we may escape them, by flying for refuge to his free mercy in Christ. Take heed of fostering any thoughts that God hath absolutely decreed to show no saving mercy to you, or that you have already committed the unpardonable sin; or that it is in vain for you to attempt the work of believing because God will not help you in it. If such thoughts prevail in your hearts, they will do you more hurt than the most blasphemous thoughts that terrify you, or any of the grossest abominations that ever you were guilty of, because they obstruct your believing on Christ for salvation. "The spirit and the bride say, come." Christ saith, "Whosoever will let him take the water of life freely" (Rev. 22:17). Therefore we are to abandon all thoughts that hinder our coming to Christ as very sinful and pernicious, arising in us from our own corruptions and Satan's delusions, and utterly opposite to the mind of Christ and the teachings of the Spirit. And what ground can we have to entertain such unbelieving thoughts? Hath God made us of his privy-council that we should be able to know that God hath decreed us to damnation, before it be manifest by our final unbelief and impenitence? As for the unpardonable sin, it consisteth in renouncing the way of salvation by Christ with the whole heart after we have attained to the knowledge of it and are convinced of the truth of it by that gospel. It is the sin that the Christian Hebrews would have been guilty of, if they had revolted from Christianity to the religion of the unbelieving Jews, that accounted Christ to be an imposter and were most rancorous persecutors of him and his ways (Heb. 6:4, 5). They that have committed that sin continue implacable, malicious enemies to Christ and his ways to the end, without any repentance. Therefore, if you can but find that you desire seriously to get an interest in Christ, and to be better Christians than you are; if you be troubled and grieved that your hearts and lives are so wicked, and that you want faith, love, and true obedience; yea, if your hearts be not maliciously bent to persecute the gospel and prefer atheism, licentiousness, or any false religion before it, you have no cause to suspect yourselves to be guilty of this unpardonable sin.

6. Add to all these "a full persuasion of the incomparable glorious excellency of Christ, and the way of salvation by him." You are to esteem the enjoyment of Christ as the only salvation and true happiness, and such an happiness as hath in it unsearchable riches of glory, and will make our cup to run over with exceeding abundance of peace and joy and glory to all eternity. We must account all things but loss for the excellency of the knowledge of Christ Jesus our Lord (Phil. 3:8). Such a persuasion as this will allure and incline your wills and affections to choose and embrace Christ as the chief good, and never to rest satisfied without the enjoyment of him, and to reject every thing that stands in competition with him or the enjoyment of him. Christ is precious in the esteem of all true believers (1 Pet. 2:7). Their

high esteem of his incomparable preciousness and excellency induceth them to sell all, that they may buy this pearl of great price (Matt. 13:46). This maketh them to say, "Lord, evermore give us this bread, that cometh down from heaven, and giveth life to the world. Lord, to whom shall we go? thou hast the words of eternal life" (John 6:32, 33, 34, 68). Because of the savor of his good ointments, his name is as ointment poured forth; therefore do the virgins love him (Song of Songs 1:3). They are sick of love to him, because he is, in their eyes, the chiefest among ten thousand (Song of Songs 5:8, 10). As the glory of God that appeared in the wonderful beauty of the Temple, and in the wisdom and glory of Solomon, drew worshipers to God from the utmost parts of the earth, so the unparalleled excellency of Christ, which was prefigured by the glory of Solomon and the Temple, doth more powerfully draw believers in these gospel days. The devil, who is the god of this world, knows how necessary it is for our salvation to discern all the glory and excellency of Christ? And therefore where the gospel is preached he maketh it his great work to eclipse the glory of Christ's ministry, and to blind the minds of the people, lest the light of his glorious gospel should shine unto them (2 Cor. 4:4).

One that is convinced of the truth of the gospel may be averse to the embracing of it until he sees also the goodness of it, that Christ is altogether lovely and excellent.

I come now to the "second principal act of faith whereby Christ himself, and his Spirit, and all his saving benefits, are actually received into the heart, which is believing on Christ, as revealed and freely promised to us in the gospel, for all his salvation." The Spirit of God doth habitually dispose and incline our hearts to a right performance of this act by enabling us to perform the first act, according to the former instructions, by believing assuredly those great things of the gospel whereby we are delivered into a form of doctrine (Rom. 6:17), which we are to obey from our hearts, and to follow as our pattern in the manner of our acting faith in Christ for our salvation. Therefore I need only exhort you briefly to act your faith in Christ according to that form and pattern in which you have been already so largely instructed. You are to believe in Christ, as alone sufficient, and as being all-sufficient for your happiness and salvation; despairing altogether of any attainment of happiness by your own wisdom, strength, works of righteousness, or any fleshly, worldly confidences whatsoever. We must be as dead people to all other confidences, and account them to be loss for Christ, according to the example of the blessed apostle (Phil. 3:3, 7, 8). We must not be grieved that we have nothing to trust upon besides Christ for our salvation; but rather we are to rejoice that we need nothing else, and that we have a sure foundation to rely upon, incomparably better than any other that can be imagined. And we must resolve to cast the burden of our souls wholly on Christ, and to seek salvation no other way, whatsoever becomes of us. If the cripple lay not the whole weight of his body upon a strong staff, but part of it on a rotten one, he is like to receive a fall. If the swimmer will not commit his body wholly to the water to bear him up, but catch at weeds, or struggle to feel out ground, he may sink to the bottom. Christ will be all our salvation, or nothing. If we seek to be saved any other way, as the Galatians did by circumcision, Christ will profit us nothing (Gal. 5:2).

You are also to receive Christ merely as a free gift, given to the chief of sinners, resolving that you will not perform any conditions to procure yourselves a right and title to him; but that you will come to him as a lost sinner, an ungodly creature, trusting on him that justifieth the ungodly; and that you will buy him without money, and without any price whatsoever (Rom. 4:5; Isa. 54:2). Look not on your own faith or love or any good qualifications in yourselves as the ground of your trusting in Christ, but only to the free grace and loving-kindness of God in Christ: "How excellent is thy loving-kindness, O God, therefore the children of men put their trust under the shadow of thy wings" (Ps. 36:7). For, if you make your faith, love, or good qualifications to be your first and principal foundation, and you build Christ upon them instead of building all upon him, you invert the order of the gospel and he will profit you nothing.

Another thing to be observed diligently is that you must come to Christ for a new holy heart and life and all things necessary thereunto, as well as for deliverance from the wrath of God and the torments of hell. You must also come to him with an ardent love and affection, and esteem him better than a thousand worlds and the only excellent portion, loathing and abhorring yourself as a vile, sinful, and miserable creature, and accounting all things dung in comparison of his excellency, that you may be able to say from the bottom of your heart, "Whom have I in heaven but thee, and there is none upon earth that I desire besides thee" (Ps. 73:25).

Lastly, you must endeavor to draw near

with full assurance of faith (Heb. 10:22), trusting on Christ constantly for your own particular salvation, upon the account of that general promise that whosoever believeth on him shall not be ashamed (Rom. 9:33). You must check yourselves for all doubtings, fears, staggerings, concerning your own salvation by Christ, saying with the psalmist, "Why art thou cast down, O my soul?" (Ps. 43:11).

The third thing contained in this direction is the avoiding all delay in the performance of this great work of believing in Christ. Until we have performed it, we continue under the power of sin and Satan and under the wrath of God; and there is nothing between hell and us besides the breath of our nostrils. It is dangerous for Lot to linger in Sodom, lest fire and brimstone come down from heaven upon him. The manslayer must flee with all haste to the city of refuge, lest the avenger of blood pursue him while his heart is hot, and slay him (Deut. 19:5, 6). We should make haste and not delay to keep God's commandments (Ps. 119:60), and flee for refuge to the hope set before us (Heb. 6:18). And God commandeth us to flee thus by faith, without which it is impossible to please God in other duties. The work is of such a nature that it may be performed as soon as you hear the gospel. "As soon as they hear of me, they shall obey me'' (Ps. 18:44). "As soon as Zion travailed, she brought forth her children'' (Isa. 66:8). We have many examples of those who receive the word by faith at the first hearing of it. Three thousand were added to the Church on the very same day wherein Peter first published the gospel in Jerusalem (Acts. 2:41). So many Jews and Gentiles were converted at the first hearing of the Apostle Paul at Antioch (Acts 13:48). The jailer and all his house believed and were baptized the same night wherein Paul first preached to them (Acts 16:33, 34). The gospel came at first to the Thessalonians, "not in word only, but in power, and in the Holy Ghost'' (1 Thess. 1:5, 6). If God open the hearts of his people to attend diligently, they may be instructed in the knowledge of the gospel by one brief sermon, sufficiently to begin the practise of saving faith. And when they know their duty, God requireth immediate performance, without allowing us the least respite in the state of unbelief. When Satan can not prevail with people to reject wholly the duty of believing, his next attempt for the ruin of their souls is to prevail with them at least to delay and shift off the performance of it from time to time, by several false reasonings and imaginations which he putteth into their minds. The most ignorant and sensual are easily prevailed with to defer this duty, until they have taken their fill of the pleasures, profits, and honors of this world, and are summoned to prepare for another by infirmities, age, sickness, praying and hoping that a large time of repentance will be granted unto them before they die. But such delays show that they are really unwilling to repent and believe, until they are forced by necessity; and that they prefer the pleasures, profits, and honors of the world above God, and Christ, and their own souls. Thus they unfit themselves more and more for this great duty, by their customary walking in sin and by misspending the precious time of their health and strength, which is most meet for the performance of this great work. They highly provoke God never to give them time or grace to repent hereafter. Others imagine, that, after they have heard the gospel of salvation by Christ, they may lawfully defer the believing it until they have sufficiently examined the truth of some other different doctrine, or until God be pleased to afford them some other means to assure them fully of the truth of the gospel. Thus they that are called seekers misspend the day of grace, "ever learning, but never coming to the knowledge of the truth" (2 Tim. 3:7).

But the truth of the gospel doth so clearly evidence itself by its own light that, if people do not wilfully shut their eyes or blind themselves by their own pride and love of their lusts, they would easily perceive that it is the truth of God; because the image of his grace, mercy, power, justice, and holiness appears manifestly engraven upon it. It is a sign people are proud, when they consent not to the words of our Lord Jesus Christ and to the doctrine which is according to godliness (2 Tim. 6:3). If they were humble and sincerely inclined to do the will of God, they would know whether the doctrine be of God or no (John 7:17), they would quickly be persuaded of the truth by Moses and the prophets, Christ and the apostles, spoken to them in the Scripture. And if they will not hear them, neither will they be persuaded tho one rose from the dead, or whatever other miracle be wrought to confirm the divine authority of the gospel (Luke 16:31). Another sort of people there are, that delay the great work of believing to the ruin of their souls, resting in an attendance upon the outward means of grace and salvation, instead of any endeavors to receive Christ by faith, tho they be convinced of the truth of the gospel. This they call waiting upon God at the doors of his grace and salvation, in the use of means appointed by him, and sitting under the droppings of the sanctuary. But let them know that this is not the right waiting on God required in Scripture. It is rather disobedience to God and to the means of his appointment, who requires that we should be doers of the word, and not hearers only, "deceiving ourselves" (James 1:22), and that we should come into the spiritual feast (Luke 14:23), and not only stand at the door or sit under the droppings of the house of God, lest Christ repute us no better than eaves-droppers. That wholly waiting on the Lord commended to us in Scripture is ever accompanied with believing and hoping in the Lord, and dependeth thereon: "I had fainted, unless I had believed to see the goodness of the Lord in the land of the living. Wait on the Lord; be of good courage, and he shall strengthen thine heart; wait, I say, on the Lord" (Ps. 27:13, 14). "It is good that a man should both hope and quietly wait for the salvation of the Lord" (Lam. 3:26). What is it that these deluded ones wait for before they perform the duty of believing? Is it for more knowledge of the gospel? The way to increase thy knowledge, as well as any other talent, is to make use of what thou hast received already. Believe heartily on Christ for all thy salvation, according to that little knowledge of the gospel which thou hast, and thou wilt have an interest in the promise of knowledge contained in the new covenant: "They shall all know me, from the least to the greatest of them, saith the Lord" (Jer. 31:34). Is it for the appointed time of thy conversion that thou waitest? Then thou waitest as those impotent folk that lay at the pool of Bethesda, waiting for the season when the angel will come down and move the water. Know then, that if you enter into Christ now by faith, thou shalt find in him waters of life and the Spirit moving them for the healing and quickening of thy soul. God hath appointed by his Word that it shall be thy duty to endeavor that the present time should be the time of thy conversion: As the Holy Ghost saith, "To-day, if thou wilt hear his voice, harden not thy heart" (Heb. 3:7, 8). And thou shall never know at what time God had purposed in his secret council to give faith to thee, until thou dost actually believe. Dost thou wait for any manifestations or flowings in of God's saving love to thy soul? Then the way to obtain it is to believe that the God of hope may fill thee with all joy and peace in believing (Rom. 15:13). Thou hast sufficient manifestation of God's love to thy soul, by the free promises of life and salvation by Christ. Do but trust on the name of the Lord, and stay upon thy God, when thou walkest in darkness, and seest no light of sensible comforts any other way; otherwise thou waitest for comfort in vain, and this shalt thou have at the Lord's hand, "thou shalt lie down in sorrow" (Isa. 50:10, 11). Dost thou wait for any qualifications to prepare thee for the work of believing? If they be good and holy qualifications, thou canst not have them before faith, but they are rather included in the nature of faith or they are fruits of it, as hath been largely proved. If they be bad and sinful, it is strange that any should wait for them, and yet no more strange than true. Some foolishly wait to be terrified with a sense of God's wrath and despairing thoughts; and these they call the pangs of the new birth; tho in their own nature they are rather the pangs of the spiritual death, and bring forth hatred to God rather than holiness, and therefore we should strive to prevent them by believing God's love in Christ, rather than to wait for them. It is true, God maketh these despairing thoughts, as well as other sins, work for good to them that are delivered from them by faith in Christ; they are moved thereby to hate sin, and to prize him the more and the comforts of his gospel, and to loath and abhor themselves: yet many are brought to him without them, by God's giving them the knowledge of their own sins and of Christ's salvation together. Several examples of these were above mentioned, who received the word with joy at the first hearing of it. And we must not desire or wait for any evil of sin, such as these despairing thoughts are, that good may come of it: neither should we expect to be worse before we be better, when we may and ought to be better presently, by believing on Christ.

The fourth thing in the direction is, that we should continue and increase in the most holy faith. And, that we may, we must not think that when we have once attained to the grace of saving faith, and thereby are begotten anew in Christ, our names are up in heaven, and therefore we may be careless; but as long as we continue in this life, we must endeavor to continue in the faith, grounded and settled, not moved away from the hope of the gospel (Col. 1:23), and to hold the beginning of our confidence, and the rejoicing of hope, stedfast to the end (Heb. 3:6, 14), and to build up ourselves in our most holy faith (Jude, verse 20), abounding therein with thanksgiving (Col. 2:7). Tho we receive Christ freely by faith; yet we are but babes in him (1 Cor. 3:1). And we must not account that we have already attained, or are already perfect (Phil. 3:12, 13), but we must strive to be more rooted and built up in him, until we come unto a "perfect man, unto the measure of the stature of the fulness of Christ" (Eph. 4:13). If the new nature be really in us by regeneration, it will have an appetite to its own continuance and increase until it come to perfection, as the new born babe (1 Pet. 2:2). And we are not only to receive Christ and a new holy nature by faith; but also to live and walk by it, and to resist the devil, and to quench all his fiery darts by it, and also to grow in grace and to perfect holiness in the fear of God; for we are kept by the mighty power of God through faith unto salvation (1 Pet. 1:5). As all our Christian warfare is the good fight of faith (1 Tim. 6:12), all spiritual life and holiness continue, grow, or decay in us, according as faith continueth, groweth, or decayeth in vigor; but when this faith beginneth to sink by fears and doubtings, the man himself beginneth to sink togther with it (Matt. 14:29, 31). Faith is like the hand of Moses: while it is held up Israel prevails; when it is let down, Amalek prevails (Ex. 17:11). This continuance and growth in faith will require our labor and industry, as well as the beginning; tho we are to ascribe the glory of all to the grace of God in Christ, who is the finisher, as well as the author of it (Heb. 12:2). The Church meeteth with great difficulties in her marching through the wilderness of this world to the heavenly Canaan, as well as in her first deliverance from Egyptian bondage; yea, we often meet with greater difficulties in going to perfection than we did in the beginning of the good work; the wisdom and mercy of God so ordering it, that we shall be exercised with the sharpest dispensations of providence and the fiercest assaults of our own corruptions and Satan's temptations, after we have grace given us to stand in the evil day. You must therefore endeavor to continue and go on in the same right manner as I have taught you to begin this great work of believing in Christ, that your faith may be of the same nature from the beginning to the end, tho it increase in degrees: for our faith is imperfect, and joined with much unbelief in this world; and we have need to pray still, "Lord, I believe, help thou mine unbelief" (Mark 9:24), and therefore we have need to strive for more faith that we may receive Christ in greater perfection. If you find your faith hath produced good works, you should thereby increase your confidence in Christ for salvation by his mere grace. But take heed of changing the nature of your faith, from trusting on the grace and merits of Christ to trusting on your own works according to the Roman doctrine. That our first justification is by grace and faith only, but our second justification is also by works. Beware also of trusting on faith itself as a work of righteousness, instead of trusting on Christ by faith. If you do not find that your believing in such a right manner as I have described doth produce such fruits of holiness as you desire, you ought not to diminish but rather to increase your confidence in him; knowing that the weakness of your faith hindereth its fruitfulness; and the greater your confidence is concerning the love of God to you in him, the greater will be your love to God and to his service. If you fall into any gross sin after the work is begun in you, as David and Peter did, think not that you must cast away your confidence and expect nothing but wrath from God and Christ, and that you must refuse to be comforted by his grace, at least for some time; for thus you would be the more weak, and prone to fall into other sins; but rather strive to believe more confidently that you have an advocate with the Father, Jesus Christ the righteous: and that he is the propitiation for our sins (1 John 2:1, 2). And let not the guilt of sin stay at all upon your conscience, but wash it away with all speed, in the fountain of Christ's blood, which is opened for us, that it may be ready for our use on all such incidental occasions; that so you may be humbled for your sins in a gospel way, and may hate your own sinfulness, and be sorry for it with godly sorrow, out of love to God. Peter might have been ruined forever by denying Christ, as Judas was by betraying him, if Peter's faith had not been upheld by Christ's prayer (Luke 21: 31, 32). If a cloud be cast over all your inward qualifications, so that you can see no grace at all in yourselves, yet still trust on him that justifieth the ungodly and came to seek and to save them that are lost. If God seem to deal with you as an enemy, by bringing on you some horrible affliction, as he did upon Job, beware of condemning your faith and its fruits, as if they were not acceptable to God: but rather say with holy Job, "Though he slay me, yet will I trust in him; but I will maintain mine own ways before him" (Job 13: 15). Strive to keep and to increase faith by faith, *i.e.*, by acting faith frequently, by trusting on God to keep and to increase it, being confident that "he who hath begun a good work in you, will perform it until the day of Jesus Christ" (Phil. 1: 6).

SELECTIONS FROM

Grace Abounding to the Chief of Sinners

BY

JOHN BUNYAN

Used in connection "God and John Bunyan; The Story of a Tinker's Triumph Through Grace."
Kenosha
Feb 5. 1922

JOHN BUNYAN

Son of a "braseyer" (hence the term "tinker"), was born at Harrowden, in the parish of Elstow, November, 1628; died in London, August 31, 1688. In 1644 Bunyan was drafted into the army, and took part in the civil war between Roundhead and Royalist. On the disbanding of the army, Bunyan returned to Elstow, and about 1649 married. He joined the Gifford Christian fellowship in 1653, and about 1655 was asked by the brethren to address them in their church gatherings. This led to his preaching in the villages round Bedford, and in 1656 he was brought into discussion with the followers of George Fox; his first book, "Some Gospel Truths Opened," was published against the Quakers in 1656. From 1660 to 1672 he was in prison and wrote "Profitable Meditations," "Praying in the Spirit," "Christian Behaviour," "The Holy City," "The Resurrection of the Dead," "Grace Abounding," and some smaller works. When released, he was chosen by the church to which he belonged as their pastor. Three years later the Declaration of Indulgence was canceled, and the licenses of the Nonconformist preachers were recalled. On March 4th, a warrant was issued for his arrest, and Bunyan was sent to prison for six months in the town jail on Bedford Bridge. During this imprisonment he wrote the first part of his memorable work, the "Pilgrim's Progress" (published 1678). This was followed by the "Life and Death of Mr. Badman" (in 1680); the "Holy War," his most memorable work after the "Pilgrim's Progress" (in 1682); and by the second part of the "Pilgrim" (the story of Christiana and her children, in 1684). Bunyan will be best remembered by his "Grace Abounding," "Holy War," and "Pilgrim's Progress," and the best of all by the last.

Bunyan's Conversion, and the Peculiar Temptations Which Followed It

1648-1650

[Bunyan begins his "Grace Abounding" with an account of his "youthful ungodliness" and his "various forms of self-righteous experience." Then comes the account of his conversion, as follows.]

Upon a day, the good providence of God called me to Bedford, to work at my calling; and in one of the streets of that town I came where there were three or four poor women sitting at a door, in the sun, talking about the things of God. And being now willing to hear their discourse, I drew near to hear what they said; for I was now a brisk talker myself in the matters of religion. But they were far above my reach. Their talk was about a new birth, the work of God in their hearts; as also how they were convinced of their miserable state by nature. They talked how God had visited their souls with his love in the Lord Jesus, and with what words and promises they had been refreshed, comforted, and supported against the temptations of the devil. Moreover, they reasoned of the suggestions and temptations of Satan in particular; and told each other, by what means they had been afflicted; and how they were borne up under his assaults. They also discoursed of their own wretchedness of heart, and of their unbelief; and did contemn, slight, and abhor their own righteousness as filthy and insufficient to do them any good.

And methought they spake as if joy did make them speak. They spake with such pleasantness of Scripture language, and with such appearance of grace in all they said, that they were to me as if they had found a new world; as if they were "people that dwelt alone, and were not to be reckoned among their neighbors" (Num. 23:9).

At this I felt my own heart began to shake and mistrust my own condition. For I saw that in all my thoughts about religion and salvation the new birth did never enter into my mind; neither knew I the comfort of the word and promise, nor the deceitfulness and treachery of my own wicked heart. As for secret thoughts, I took no notice of them; neither did I understand what Satan's temptations were, nor how they were to be withstood.

Thus, therefore, when I had heard and considered what they said, I left them, and went about my employment again; but my heart would tarry with them. For I was greatly affected with their words; because by them

I was convinced that I wanted the true tokens of a truly godly man, and also because I was convinced of the happy and blessed condition of him that was such a one.

Therefore I would often make it my business to be going again and again into the company of these poor people, for I could not stay away. And the more I went among them, the more I did question my condition. And, as I still do remember, presently I found two things within me, at which I did sometimes marvel; especially considering what a blind, ignorant, sordid, and ungodly wretch but just before I was. The one was, a very great softness and tenderness of heart, which caused me to fall under the conviction of what by Scripture they asserted; and the other was a bending in my mind, a continual meditating on it, and on all other good things which at that time I heard or read of. By these things my mind was now so turned that it lay, like a horse-leech at the vein, still crying out, "Give, give" (Prov. 30:15). It was so fixt on eternity and on the things about the kingdom of heaven (that is, so far as I knew, tho as yet, God knows, I knew but little) that neither pleasures, nor profits, nor persuasions, nor threats could make it let go its hold; and tho I speak it with shame, yet it is a certain truth, it would then have been

7

as difficult for me to have taken my mind from heaven to earth as I have found it often since to get it again from earth to heaven.

One thing I may not omit. There was a young man in our town, to whom my heart before was knit more than to any other; but he being a most wicked creature for cursing and swearing and whoring, I now shook him off and forsook his company. About a quarter of a year after I had left him, I met him in a certain lane, and asked him how he did. He, after his old swearing and mad way, answered he was well. "But Harry," said I, "why do you curse and swear thus? What will become of you, if you die in this condition?" He answered me in a great chafe, "What would the devil do for company, if it was not for such as I am?"

About this time I met with some Ranters' books,[1] which were highly in esteem by several old professors. Some of these I read, but was not able to make any judgment about them. Wherefore as I read in them and thought upon them, seeing myself unable to judge, I would betake myself to a hearty prayer in this manner: "O Lord, I am a fool, and not able to know the truth from error. Lord,

[1] The Ranters were Familists—a mystic sect, who, under the seductive name of "The Family of Love," concealed the worst tenets of Antinomianism.—J. N. B.

leave me not in my own blindness, either to approve of or condemn this doctrine; if it be of God, let me not despise it; if it be of the devil, let me not embrace it. Lord, I lay my soul in this matter, only at thy foot; let me not be deceived I humbly beseech thee."
I had one religious intimate companion all this while, and that was a poor man; but about this time, he also turned a most devilish Ranter, and gave himself up to all manner of filthiness, especially uncleanness; he would also deny that there was a God, angel, or spirit; and would laugh at all exhortations to sobriety. When I labored to rebuke his wickedness, he would laugh the more, and pretend that he had gone through all religions, and could never hit upon the right till now. Wherefore abominating those cursed principles, I left his company forthwith, and became to him as great a stranger as I had been before a familiar.

Neither was this man only a temptation to me; but my calling lying in the country, I happened to come into several people's company, who tho strict in religion formerly, yet were also drawn away by these Ranters. These would also talk with me of their ways, and condemn me as legal and dark; pretending that they only had attained to perfection, that they could do what they would and not sin. Oh! these temptations were suitable to my flesh, I being but a young man, and my nature in its prime; but God, who had, as I hope, designed me for better things, kept me in the fear of his name and did not suffer me to accept such cursed principles. And blessed be God, who put it into my heart to cry to him to be kept and directed, still distrusting mine own wisdom; for I have since seen even the effects of that prayer in his preserving me, not only from ranting errors, but from those also that have sprung up since. The Bible was precious to me in those days.

And now I began to look into the Bible with new eyes; and especially the epistles of the Apostle Paul were sweet and pleasant to me. And then I was never out of the Bible, either by reading or meditation; still crying out to God that I might know the truth and the way to heaven and glory.

But as I went on and read, I hit upon the passage, "To one is given by the Spirit the word of wisdom; to another the word of knowledge by the same Spirit; and to another faith," etc. (1 Cor. 12:8). And tho as I have since seen, that by this scripture the Holy Ghost intends, in special, things extraordinary; yet on me it did then fasten with conviction, that I did want things ordinary, even that understanding and wisdom that other Christians had. On this passage I mused, and could not tell what to do. Especially this word faith put me to it; for I could not help it, but sometimes must question, whether I had any faith or no; but I was loath to conclude I had no faith; for if I do so, thought I, then I shall count myself a very castaway indeed. "No," said I with myself, "tho I am an ignorant sot, and want those blessed gifts of knowledge and understanding that other people have, yet at a venture I will conclude I am not altogether faithless, tho I know not what faith is." For it was shown me, and that too (as I have seen since) by Satan, that those who conclude themselves in a faithless state have neither rest nor quiet in their souls; and I was loath to fall quite into despair. Wherefore, by this suggestion, I was made afraid to see my want of faith.

But God would not suffer me thus to destroy my soul, but did, against this my sad and blind conclusion, create within me such suppositions that I could not rest content until I did come to some certain knowledge whether I had faith or not; this always running in my mind, "But how if you want faith indeed? But how can you tell you have faith?" And besides, I saw for certain if I had not, I was sure to perish forever. So that tho I endeavored at the first to look over the business of faith, yet in a little time, I better considering the matter, was willing to put myself upon the trial whether I had faith or no. But alas! so ignorant was I, poor wretch, that I knew no more how to do it than I knew how to begin and accomplish that rare and curious piece of art which I never yet saw or considered.

Wherefore while I was thus considering (for you must know that as yet I had not in this matter broken my mind to any one, only did hear and consider), the tempter came in with this delusion, "That there was no way for me to know I had faith but by trying to work some miracles"; urging those scriptures that seemed to enforce and strengthen his temptation. Nay, one day, as I was between Elstow and Bedford, the temptation was hot upon me to try if I had faith by doing some miracle; which miracle at this time was this —I must say to the puddles that were in the horse-pads, "Be dry," and to the dry places, "Be ye puddles." And truly one time I was going to say so indeed; but just as I was about to speak, this thought came into my mind; "But go under yonder hedge, and pray first that God would make you able." But when I had concluded to pray, this came hot upon me—that if I prayed, and came again and tried to do it, and yet did nothing notwithstanding, then to be sure I had no faith, but was a castaway and lost. Nay, thought I, if it be so, I will not try yet, but will stay a little longer.

So I continued at a great loss; for I thought if they only had faith who could do so wonderful things, then I concluded that I neither had it, nor yet was ever like to have it. Thus I was tossed betwixt the devil and my own ignorance, and so perplexed that I could not tell what to do.

About this time, the state and happiness of these poor people at Bedford was thus, in a kind of a vision, presented to me. I saw, as if they were on the sunny side of some high mountain, there refreshing themselves with the pleasant beams of the sun, while I was shivering and shrinking in the cold, afflicted with frost, snow, and dark clouds. Methought also betwixt me and them, I saw a wall that did compass about this mountain. Now through this wall my soul did greatly desire to pass; concluding that if I could, I would there also comfort myself with the heat of their sun. About this wall I bethought myself to go again and again, still praying as I went, to see if I could find some way or passage by which I might enter therein; but none could I find for some time; at the last I saw as it were, a narrow gap, like a little doorway in the wall, through which I attempted to pass. Now the passage being very strait and narrow, I made many efforts to get in, but all in vain; at last with great striving, methought I at first did get in my head, and after that, by a sidelong striving, my shoulders, and my whole body; then I was exceeding glad, and went and sat down in the midst of them, and so was comforted with the light and heat of their sun.

Now this mountain and wall was thus made out to me. The mountain signified the Church of the living God; the sun that shone thereon, the shining of his merciful face on them that were therein; the wall I thought was the world, that did make separation between the Christians and the world; and the gap which was in the wall, I thought was Jesus Christ, who is the way to God the Father (John 14:6). But as the passage was wonderful narrow, even so narrow that I could not but with great difficulty enter in thereat, it showed me that none could enter into life but those that were in downright earnest, and left the wicked world behind them; for here was only room for body and soul, but not for body and soul and sin (Matt. 7:14).

This resemblance abode upon my spirit many days; all which time I saw myself in a forlorn and sad condition, but yet was provoked to vehement hunger and desire to be one of that number that did sit in the sunshine. Now also would I pray wherever I was, whether at home or abroad, in house or field; and would also often, with lifting up of heart, sing that of the fifty-first psalm, "O Lord consider my distress"; for as yet I knew not where I was.

Neither as yet could I attain to any comfortable persuasion that I had faith in Christ; but instead, I began to find my soul assaulted with fresh doubts about my future happiness; especially with such as these, "Whether I was elected? But how if the day of grace should now be past and gone?" By these two temptations I was very much afflicted and disquieted; sometimes by the one, and sometimes by the other of them.

And first, to speak of that about my questioning my election, I found that, tho I was in a flame to find the way to heaven and glory, and nothing could beat me off from this, yet this question did so discourage me that I was, especially sometimes, as if the very strength of my body had been taken away by the force and power thereof. This scripture did also seem to me to trample upon all my desires: "It is neither of him that willeth, nor of him that runneth; but of God that showeth mercy" (Rom. 9). With this scripture I could not tell what to do. For I evidently saw, that unless God had voluntarily chosen me to be a vessel of mercy, tho I should desire and long and labor until my heart did break, no good could come of it. Therefore this would stick with me, "How can you tell that you are elected? and what if you should not be? How then?" "O Lord," thought I, "what if I should not, indeed!" "It may be you ar not," said the tempter; "it may be so, in deed," thought I. "Why then," said Satan "you had as good leave off, and strive n further; for if indeed you should not b elected and chosen of God, there is no hop of your being saved. For it is neither of hi that willeth, nor of him that runneth; but o God, that showeth mercy." By these thing I was driven to my wit's end, not knowin what to say, or how to answer these tempta- tions. Indeed, I little thought that Satan ha thus assaulted me, but that rather it was m own prudence thus to start the question. Fo that the elect only obtained eternal life, tha I without scruple did heartily close withal but that myself was one of them, there la the question.

Thus therefore, for several days, I w greatly perplexed, and as often ready to s with faintness in my mind. But one day, a I had been many weeks opprest and c down therewith, as I was giving up the ghost of all my hopes of ever attaining life, that sentence fell with weight upon my spirit, "Look at the generations of old and see: did ever any trust in God, and were confounded?" At which I was greatly encouraged in my soul. For thus, at that very instant it was expounded to me: "Begin at the beginning of Genesis, and read to the end of the Revelations, and see if you can find that there was ever any that trusted in the Lord and was confounded." So coming home, I presently went to my Bible, to see if I could find that saying, not doubting but to find it presently; for it was with such strength and comfort on my spirit that I was as if it talked with me. Well, I looked, but I found it not; only it abode upon me. Then did I ask first this good man and then another if they knew where it was, but they knew no such place. And at this I wondered, that such a sentence should so suddenly, and with such comfort and strength, seize and abide upon my heart; and yet that none could find it (for I doubted not that it was in the Holy Scriptures). Thus continued above a year, and could not find e place; but at last, casting my eyes upon e Apocryphal books, I found it in Ecclesi-icus 2:10. This, at the first, did somewhat unt me, because it was not in those texts that we call holy and canonical; yet, as this sentence was the sum and substance of many of the promises, it was my duty to take the comfort of it; and I bless God for that word, for it was of good to me. That word doth still ofttimes shine before my face.

After this, that other doubt did come with strength upon me, "But how if the day of grace be past and gone? How if you have overstood the time of mercy?" Now I remember that one day, as I was walking in the country, I was much in the thoughts of this, "But how if the day of grace is past?" And to aggravate my trouble, the tempter presented to my mind those good people of Bedford, and suggested thus unto me, That these being converted already, they were all that God would save in those parts; and that I came too late, for these had got the blessing before I came. Now I was in great distress, thinking in very deed that this might well be so. Wherefore I went up and down, bemoaning my sad condition for standing off thus long, and spending so many years in sin as I had done, still crying out, "Oh! that I had turned sooner! Oh! that I had turned seven years ago!" It made me also angry with myself, to think that I should have no more wit but to trifle away my time till my soul and heaven were lost!

But when I had been long vexed with this fear and was scarce able to take one step more, just about the same place where I received my other encouragement these words broke in upon my mind, "Compel them to come in, that my house may be filled"—"and yet there is room" (Luke 14:22, 23). These words, "And yet there is room," were sweet words to me; for truly I thought that when the Lord Jesus did speak these words, he then did think of me; and that he knowing that the time would come that I should be afflicted with fear that there was no place left for me in his bosom, did before speak this word and leave it upon record, that I might find help thereby against this vile temptation. This I then verily believed. In the light and encouragement of this word, I went a pretty while. And the comfort was the more when I thought that the Lord Jesus should speak those words on purpose for my sake; for I did think verily that he did on purpose speak them to encourage me withal.

But I was not without my temptations to go back again; temptations, I say, both from Satan, mine own heart, and carnal acquaintance. But I thank God these were outweighed by that sound sense of death, and of the day of judgment, which abode, as it were, continually in my view. I would often also think on Nebuchadnezzar; of whom it is said, He had given to him all the kingdoms of the earth (Dan. 5:18, 19). Yet, thought I, if this great man had all his portion in this world, one hour in hell-fire would make him forget all. Which consideration was a great help to me.

I was almost made about this time to see something concerning the beasts that Moses counted clean and unclean. I thought these beasts were types of men; the clean types of them that were the people of God; but the unclean types of such as were the children of the wicked one. Now I read, that the clean beasts "chewed the cud"; that is, thought I, they show us we must feed upon the word of God. They also "parted the hoof." I thought that signified we must part, if we would be saved, with the ways of ungodly men. And also, in further reading about them, I found, that tho we did chew the cud as the hare, yet if we walked with claws, like a dog, or if we did part the hoof, like the swine, yet if we did not chew the cud, as the sheep, we are still for all that but unclean. For I thought the hare to be a type of those that talk of the word yet walk in the ways of sin; and that the swine was like him that parteth with his outward pollution but still wanteth the work of faith, without which there could be no way of salvation, let a man be ever so devout (Deut. 14).

After this, I found by reading the word that those that must be glorified with Christ in another world must be called by him here; called to the partaking of a share in his word and righteousness, and to the comforts and first-fruits of his Spirit, which do indeed prepare the soul for that rest and the house of glory, which is in heaven above. Here again I was at a very great stand, not knowing what to do, fearing I was not called; for, thought I, "if I be not called, what then can do me good?" But oh! how I now loved those words that spake of a Christian's calling! as when the Lord said to one, "Follow me"; and to another, "Come after me." And oh! thought I, "that he would say so to me too; how gladly would I run after him!" I can not now express with what longings and breathings in my soul I cried to Christ to call me. Thus I continued for a time, all on a flame to be converted to Jesus Christ; and did also see at that day such glory in a converted state that I could not be contented without a share therein. Gold! could it have been gotten for gold, what would I have given for it! Had I had a whole world, it had all gone ten thousand times over for this, that my soul might have been in a converted state.

How lovely now was every one in my eyes that I thought to be converted men and women! They shone; they walked like a people that carried the broad seal of heaven about them. But that which made me sick was that of Christ in St. Mark, "He went up into a mountain, and called to him whom he would, and they came unto him" (Mark 3:13). This scripture made me faint and fear, yet it kindled fire in my soul. That which made me fear was this; lest Christ should have no liking to me, for he called "whom he would." But oh! the glory that I saw in that condition did still so engage my heart that I could seldom read of any that Christ did call but I presently wished, "Would I had been in their clothes; would I had been born Peter; would I had been John; or, would I had been by and heard him when he called them, how would I have cried, O Lord, call me also!" But oh! I feared he would not call me!

And truly, the Lord let me go thus many months together and showed me nothing, either that I was already, or should be called hereafter. But at last, after much time spent and many groans to God, that word came in unto me, "I will cleanse their blood that I have not cleansed; for the Lord dwelleth in Zion" (Joel 3:21). These words I thought were sent to encourage me to wait still upon

God; and signified unto me that if I were not already, yet the time might come, I might be in truth converted unto Christ.

About this time I began to break my mind to those poor people at Bedford, and to tell them my condition; which when they had heard, they told Mr. Gifford of me;[2] who himself also took occasion to talk with me, and was willing to be well persuaded of me, tho I think from little grounds. But he invited me to his house, where I would hear him confer with others about the dealings of God with their souls; from all which I still received more conviction, and from that time began to see something of the vanity and inward wretchedness of my wicked heart. For as yet I knew no great matter therein; but now it began to be discovered to me, and also to work at that rate as it never did before. Now I evidently found that lusts and corruptions put forth themselves within me in wicked thoughts and desires, which I did not regard before. My desires also for heaven and life began to fail. I found also, that whereas before, my soul was full of longing after God, now it began to hanker after every foolish vanity; yea, my heart would not be moved to mind that which was good; it began to be

[2] The Rev. John Gifford was pastor of a small congregation in Bedford.

careless, both of my soul and heaven; it would now continually hang back, both to and in every duty; and was as a clog on the leg of a bird, to hinder him from flying. Nay, thought I, "Now I grow worse and worse; now I am farther from conversion than ever I was before." Wherefore I began to sink greatly in my soul, and began to entertain such discouragement in my heart as laid me as low as hell. If now I should have burned at the stake, I could not believe that Christ had a love for me; alas! I could neither hear him, nor see him, nor feel him, nor savor any of his things; I was driven as with a tempest, my heart would be unclean, and the Canaanites would dwell in the land.

Sometimes I would tell my condition to the people of God; when they would pity me, and would tell me of the promises; but they had as good have told me that I must reach the sun with my finger as have bidden me receive or rely upon the promises; all my sense and feeling were against me; and I saw I had a heart that would sin, and that lay under a law that would condemn. These things have often made me think of the child which the father brought to Christ, who, while he was yet coming to him, was thrown down by the devil, and also so rent and torn by him, that he lay and wallowed, foaming (Luke 9:42; Mark 9:20).

Further, in these days I would find my heart to shut itself up against the Lord, and against his holy Word. I have found myself to set, as it were, the shoulder to the door, to keep him out; and that, too, even then, when I have with many a bitter sigh cried, "Good Lord, break it open! Lord, break these gates of brass, and cut these bars of iron asunder!" (Ps. 107:16). Yet that word would sometimes create in my heart a peaceable pause, "I girded thee, tho thou hast not known me" (Isa. 45:5).

But all this while, as to the act of sinning I was never more tender than now. I durst not take a pin or stick, tho but so big as a straw, for my conscience now was sore and would smart at every touch. I could not now tell how to speak my words for fear I should misplace them. Oh, how cautiously did I then go in all I did or said! I found myself as in a miry bog that shook if I did but stir; and was, as there, left both of God, and Christ, and the Spirit, and all good things.

But, I observed, tho I was such a great sinner before conversion, yet God never much charged the guilt of the sins of my ignorance upon me; only he showed me I was lost if I had not Christ, because I had been a sinner. I saw that I wanted a perfect righteousness to present me without fault before God, and this righteousness was nowhere to be found but in the person of Jesus Christ.

But my original and inward pollution! That, that was my plague and affliction; that I had the guilt of, to amazement; by reason of that I was more loathsome in my own eyes than a toad, and thought I was so in God's eyes too. Sin and corruption, I said, would as naturally bubble out of my heart as water would out of a fountain. I thought now that every one had a better heart than I had. I could have changed heart with any body. I thought none but the devil himself could equal me for inward wickedness and pollution of mind. I fell therefore at the sight of my own vileness deeply into despair; for I concluded that this condition that I was in could not stand with a state of grace. "Sure," thought I, "I am forsaken of God; sure I am given up to the devil and to a reprobate mind"; and thus I continued a long while, even for some two years together.

While I was thus afflicted with the fears of my own damnation, there were two things would make me wonder. The one was when I saw old people hunting after the things of this life, as if they should live here always. The other was when I found professors much distrest and cast down, when they met with outward losses; as of husband, wife, or child, etc. "Lord," thought I, "what a seeking after carnal things by some, and what grief in others for the loss of them! If they so much labor after and shed so many tears for the things of this present life, how am I to be bemoaned, pitied, and prayed for! My soul is dying! my soul is damning! Were my soul but in a good condition, and were I but sure of it, ah! how rich should I esteem myself, tho blest with but bread and water! I should count these but small afflictions, and should bear them as little burdens." "A wounded spirit who can bear?"

But tho I was much troubled, and afflicted, with the sight and sense and terror of my own wickedness, yet I was afraid to let this sight and sense go quite off my mind. For I found that unless guilt of conscience was taken off the right way, that is, by the blood of Christ, a man grew rather worse for the loss of his trouble of mind. Wherefore if my guilt lay hard upon me, then would I cry that the blood of Christ might take it off. And if it was going off without it (for the sense of sin would be sometimes as if it would die, and go quite away), then I would also strive to fetch it upon my heart again by bringing the punishment of sin in hell-fire upon my spirit; and would cry, "Lord, let it not go off my heart but by the right way, by the blood of Christ and the application of thy mercy, through him, to my soul.'' For that Scripture did lie much upon me, ''without shedding of blood, there is no remission'' (Heb. 9:22). And that which made me the more afraid of this was because I had seen some who, tho when they were under the wounds of conscience would cry and pray, yet feeling rather present ease for their trouble than pardon for their sin, cared not how they lost their guilt, so they got it out of their mind. Now, having got it off the wrong way, it was not sanctified unto them; but they grew harder and blinder, and more wicked after their trouble. This made me afraid, and made me cry to God the more that it might not be so with me.

And now I was sorry that God had made me man, for I feared I was a reprobate. I counted man as unconverted, the most doleful of all creatures. Thus being afflicted and tossed about my sad condition, I counted myself alone and above the most of men unblest. Yea, I thought it impossible that ever I should attain to so much godliness of heart as to thank God that he had made me a man. Man, indeed, is the most noble by creation of all creatures in the visible world; but by sin he hath made himself the most ignoble. The beasts, birds, fishes—I blest their condition! for they had not a sinful nature; they were not obnoxious to the wrath of God; they were not to go to hell-fire after death. I could therefore have rejoiced had my condition been as any of theirs.

His Consolation In Christ; the Trials of His Faith; and the Means of Relief

1650-1651

In this condition I went a great while; but when the comforting time was come, I heard one preach a sermon on these words in the Song (Song 4:1), "Behold thou art fair, my love; behold thou art fair." But at that time, he made these two words, "my love," his chief and subject matter; from which after he had a little opened the text, he observed these several conclusions: 1. That the Church, and so every saved soul, is Christ's love, when loveless. 2. Christ's love, without a cause. 3. Christ's love, which hath been hated of the world. 4. Christ's love, when under temptation and under desertion. 5. Christ's love, from first to last. But I got nothing by what he said at present. Only when he came to the application of the fourth particular, this was the word he said: "If it be so, that the saved soul is Christ's love, when under temptation and desertion; then, poor tempted soul, when thou art assaulted and afflicted with temptations, and the hidings of God's face, yet think on these two words, 'My love,' still."

So as I was going home, these words came again into my thoughts; and I well remember, as they came in, I said thus in my heart, "What shall I get by thinking on these two words?" This thought had no sooner passed through my heart, but these words began to kindle in my spirit; "Thou art my love; thou art my love," twenty times together; and still as they ran in my mind they waxed stronger and warmer, and began to make me look up. But being as yet between hope and fear, I still replied in my heart, "But is it true? But is it true?" At which that sentence fell upon me, "He wist not that it was true, which was done unto him of the angel" (Acts 12:9). Then I began to give place to the word, which with power did over and over make this joyful sound within my soul, "Thou art my love, and nothing shall separate thee from my love." And with that my heart was filled full of comfort and hope, and now I could believe that my sins would be forgiven me. Yea, I was now so taken with the love and mercy of God that I remember I could not tell how to contain till I got home. I thought I could have spoken of his love, and have told of his mercy to me, even to the very crows that sat upon the plowed lands before me, had they been capable to have understood me. Wherefore I said in my soul with much gladness, "Well, would I had pen and ink here, I would write this down before I go any further; for surely I will not forget this forty years hence." But alas! within less than forty days I began to question this again; which made me begin to question all still. Yet still at times I was helped to believe that it was a true manifestation of grace unto my soul, tho I had lost much of the life and savor of it.

Now about a week or a fortnight after this, I was much followed by this scripture, "Simon, Simon, behold Satan hath desired to have you" (Luke 22:31). And sometimes it would sound so loud within me, that once above all the rest, I turned my head over my shoulder, thinking verily that some man behind me had called me, being at a great distance, methought he called so loud. It came, as I have thought since, to stir me up to prayer and watchfulness; it came to acquaint me that a cloud and a storm was coming down upon me; but I understood it not. Also, as I remember, that time that it called to me so loud was the last time that it sounded in mine ears. But methinks I hear still with what a loud voice these words, "Simon, Simon," sounded in mine ears: and altho that was not my name, yet it made me suddenly look behind me, believing that he that called so loud meant me.

But so foolish was I, and so ignorant, that I knew not the reason of this sound (which as I did both see and feel soon after, was sent from heaven as an alarm, to awaken me to provide for what was coming); only I would muse and wonder in my mind, to think what should be the reason that this scripture, and at this rate, so often and so loud, should still be sounding and rattling in mine ears. But as I said before, I soon after perceived the end of God therein.

For, about the space of a month after, a very great storm came down upon me, which handled me twenty times worse than all I had met with before. It came stealing upon me, now by one piece, then by another. First, all my comfort was taken from me; then darkness seized upon me; after which whole floods of blasphemies, both against God, Christ, and the Scriptures, were poured upon my spirit, to my great confusion and astonishment. These blasphemous thoughts were such as stirred up questions in me against the very being of a God and his only beloved Son: as whether there were in truth a God or Christ? And whether the Holy Scriptures were not rather a fable and cunning story than the holy and pure Word of God? The tempter would also much assault me with this, "How can you tell but that the Turks have as good scriptures to prove their Mahomet the Savior as we have to prove our Jesus? And could I think that so many ten thousands, in so many countries and kingdoms, should be without knowledge of the right way to heaven (if there were indeed a heaven), and that we only, who live in a corner of the earth, should alone be blest therewith? Every one doth think his own religion rightest, both Jews, and Moors, and Pagans; and how if all our faith, and Christ, and his Scriptures, should be but a think-so too?"

Sometimes I endeavored to argue against these suggestions, and to set some of the sentences of blessed Paul against them. But, alas! I quickly felt such arguings as these would return again upon me; "Tho we made so great a matter of Paul, and of his words, yet how could I tell but that in very deed he, being a subtle and cunning man, might give himself up to deceive with strong delusions, and also to take the pains and travail to undo and destroy his fellows."

These suggestions (with many others which at this time I may not and dare not utter, either by word or pen) did make such a seizure upon my spirit, and did so overpower both with their number, continuance, and fiery force, that I felt as if there were nothing else but these from morning to night within me; and as tho indeed there could be room for nothing else; and also concluded that God had in very wrath to my soul given me up to them, to be carried away with them as with a mighty whirlwind. Only by the distaste that they gave to my spirit I felt there was something in me that refused to embrace them. But this consideration I then only had when God gave me leave (as Job says) to swallow my spittle; otherwise the noise, and strength, and force of these temptations would drown and overflow, and as it were bury all such thoughts or the remembrance of any such thing.

While I was in this temptation, I often found my mind suddenly put upon it to curse and swear, or to speak some grievous thing against God, or Christ his Son, and of the Scriptures. Now, I thought, surely I am possest of the devil. At other times again, I thought I should be bereft of my wits; for in-instead of lauding and magnifying God the Lord with others, if I have but heard him spoken of, presently some most horrible, blasphemous thought or other would bolt out of my heart against him; so that whether I did think that God was, or again did think that there was no such thing, no love, nor peace, nor gracious disposition could I feel within me.

These things did sink me into very deep despair, for I concluded that such things could not possibly be found among them that love God. I often did compare myself to the case of a child whom some gipsy hath by force taken up in her arms, and is carrying from friends and country: kick sometimes I did, and also shriek and cry; but yet I was bound in the wings of the temptation, and the wind would carry me away. I thought also of King Saul and of the evil spirit that did possess him; and did greatly fear that my condition was the same with that of his (1 Sam. 16:14).

In those days, when I have heard others talk of what was the sin against the Holy Ghost, then would the tempter so provoke me to desire to sin that sin that I was as if I could not, must not, neither should be quiet until I had committed it. If it were to be committed by speaking such a word, then I have been as if my mouth would have spoken that word, whether I would or no; and in so strong a measure was the temptation upon me, that often I have been ready to clap my hands under my chin, to hold my mouth from opening; at other times, to leap with my head downward into some muckhill hole or other, to keep my mouth from speaking.

Now again I counted the state of every thing that God had made far better than this dreadful state of mine, and such as my companions were. Yet, gladly would I have been in the condition of a dog or a horse; for I knew they had no souls to perish under the everlasting weight of hell or sin, as mine was like to do. Nay, tho I saw this, and felt this, and was broken to pieces with it, yet that which added to my sorrow was that I could not find, that with all my soul I did desire deliverance. That scripture did also tear and rend my soul in the midst of these distractions: "The wicked are like the troubled sea, when it can not rest; whose waters cast up mire and dirt. There is no peace, saith my God, to the wicked" (Isa. 57:20, 21).

And now my heart was at times exceeding hard. If I would have given a thousand pounds for a tear, I could not shed one; no, nor sometimes scarce desire to shed one. I was much dejected to think that this would be my lot. I saw some could mourn and lament their sin; and others, again, could rejoice and bless God for Christ; and others again could quietly talk of and with gladness remember the Word of God; while I only was in the storm or tempest. This much sunk me. I thought my condition was alone. I would therefore much bewail my hard hap; but to get out of or get rid of these things I could not.

While this temptation lasted, which was about a year, I could attend upon none of the ordinances of God, but with sore and great affliction. Yea, then was I most distrest with blasphemies. If I had been hearing the Word, then uncleanness, blasphemies, and despair would hold me a captive there. If I had been reading, then sometimes I had sudden thoughts to question all I read; again my mind would be so strangely snatched away that I have neither known nor regarded nor remembered so much as the sentence that but now I had read. In prayer also I have been greatly troubled by Satan at this time. Sometimes I have thought I have felt him behind me, pull my clothes. He would also be continually at me in time of prayer to have done; "Break off, make haste, you have prayed enough, and stay no longer" still drawing my mind away. Sometimes also he would cast in such wicked thoughts as these, that I must pray to him and for him. I have thought sometimes of that, "Fall down," or, "if thou wilt fall down and worship me" (Matt. 4:9). Also, when because I have had wandering thoughts, I have labored to compose my mind and fix it upon God, then with great force hath the tempter labored to distract and confound me, and to turn away my mind, by presenting to my heart and fancy the form of a bush, a bull, a besom, or the like, as if I should pray to these: to these he would also (at some times especially) so hold my mind that I was as if I could think of nothing else, or pray to nothing else but to these, or such as they.

Yet at times I would have some strong and heart-affecting apprehensions of God, and the reality of the truth of his gospel. And, oh! how would my heart, at such times, put forth itself with inexpressible groanings. My whole soul was then in every word. I would cry with pangs after God, that he would be merciful unto me. But then I would be daunted again with such conceits as these—I would think that God did mock at these my prayers, saying, and that in the audience of his holy angels, "This poor, simple wretch doth hanker after me, as if I had nothing to do with my mercy but to bestow it on such as he. Alas, poor soul! how art thou deceived! It is not for such as thee to have favor with the Highest."

Then hath the tempter come upon me also with such discouragements as these. "You are very hot for mercy, but I will cool you; this frame shall not last always: many have been as hot as you for a spirit, but I have quenched their zeal." And with this, such and such who were fallen off would be set before mine eyes. Then I would be afraid that I should do so too; but thought I, I am glad this comes into my mind: well, I will watch, and take what care I can. "Tho you do," saith Satan, "I shall be too hard for you. I will cool you insensibly, by degrees, by little and little. What care I (says he) tho I be seven years in chilling your heart, if I can do it at last! Continual rocking will lull a crying child asleep. I will ply it close, but I will have my end accomplished. Tho you be burning hot at present, yet I can pull you from this fire; I shall have you cold before it be long."

These things brought me into great straits. For as I could not find myself fit for present death, so I thought, to live long, would make me more unfit; for time would make me forget all, and wear even the remembrance of the evil of sin, the worth of heaven, and the need I had of the blood of Christ to wash me, both out of mind and thought. But I thank Christ Jesus, these things did not make me slack my crying, but rather did put me more upon it (like her who met with the adulterer—Deut. 22:27). In which days that was a good word to me, after I had suffered these things awhile: "I am persuaded that neither height, nor depth, death nor life, etc., shall separate us from the love of God, which is in Christ Jesus our Lord" (Rom. 8:38, 39). And now I hoped long life would not destroy me nor make me miss of heaven.

Yet I had some supports in this temptation, tho they were then all questioned by me. That in Jer. 3:1, was something to me; and so was the consideration of verse 5, of that chapter; that tho we have spoken and done as evil things as we could, yet we shall cry unto God, "My Father, thou art the guide of my youth"; and shall return unto him. I had also once a sweet glance from that in 2 Cor. 5:21: "For he hath made him to be sin for us, who knew no sin, that we might be made the righteousness of God in him." I remember too that one day, as I was sitting in a neighbor's house, very sad at the consideration of my many blasphemies, and as I was saying in my mind, "What ground have I to think that I, who have been so vile and abominable, should ever inherit eternal life?" that word came suddenly upon me, "What shall we say to these things? If God be for us, who can be against us?" (Rom. 8:31). That also was a help to me, "Because I live, ye shall live also" (John 14:19). But these words were but hints, touches, and short visits, tho very sweet when present. Only they lasted not, but like Peter's sheet, of a sudden were caught up from me to heaven again (Acts 10:16).

But afterward the Lord did more fully and graciously discover himself unto me, and indeed did quite not only deliver me from the guilt that by these things was laid upon my conscience, but also from the very filth thereof; for the temptation was removed, and I was put into my right mind again, as other Christians were.

I remember that one day, as I was musing on the wickedness and blasphemy of my heart, and considering the enmity that was in me to God, that scripture came into my mind: "He hath made peace by the blood of his cross" (Col. 1:20). By which I was made to see, both again and again, that God and my soul were friends by his blood; yea, I saw that the justice of God and my sinful soul could embrace and kiss each other, through his blood. This was a good day to me; I hope I shall never forget it. At another time as I sat by the fire in my house, and was musing on my wretchedness, the Lord made that also a precious word unto me: "Forasmuch then as the children were partakers of flesh and blood, he also himself likewise took part of the same; that through death he might destroy him that had the power of death, that is, the devil; and deliver them who, through fear of death, were all their lifetime subject to bondage" (Heb. 2:14, 15). I thought that the glory of these words was then so weighty on me, that I was both once and twice ready to swoon as I sat; yet not with grief and trouble, but with solid joy and peace.

At this time I also sat under the ministry of holy Mr. Gifford, whose doctrine, by God's grace, was much for my stability. This man made it much his business to deliver the people of God from all those false and unsound tests, that by nature we are prone to. He would bid us take special heed that we took not up any truth upon trust; but cry mightily to God, that he would convince us of the reality thereof, and set us down therein by his own Spirit in the holy word. "For," said he, "if you do otherwise, when temptation comes, if strongly, you not having received them with evidence from heaven, will find you want that help and strength now to resist that once you thought you had." This was as seasonable to my soul as the former and latter rains in their seasons. For I have found, and that by sad experience, the truth of these his words. For I had felt, no man can say, especially when tempted by the devil, that Jesus Christ is Lord, but by the Holy Ghost. Wherefore I found my soul through grace very apt to drink in this doctrine, and to incline to pray to God, that in nothing that pertained to God's glory and my own eternal happiness he would suffer me to be without the confirmation thereof from heaven. For now I saw clearly the difference betwixt the notion of flesh and blood and the revelation of God in heaven: also a great difference betwixt that faith that is feigned and according to man's wisdom, and that which comes by a man's being born thereunto of God (Matt. 16:15; 1 John 5:1).

But oh! now, how was my soul led from truth to truth by God! Even from the birth and cradle of the Son of God to his ascension and second coming from heaven to judge the world. Truly, I then found, upon this account, the great God was very good unto me. For, to my remembrance, there was not any thing that I then cried unto God to make known and reveal unto me, but he was pleased to do it for me. I mean, not one part of the gospel of the Lord Jesus, but I was orderly led into it. Methought I saw with great evidence, from the four evangelists, the wonderful works of God in giving Jesus Christ to save us, from his conception and birth even to his second coming to judgment. Methought I was as if I had seen him born, as if I had seen him grow up; as if I had seen him walk through this world from the cradle to the cross: to which also, when he came, I saw how gently he gave himself to be hanged and nailed on it, for my sins and wicked doing. Also as I was musing on this his progress, that dropt on my spirit: "He was ordained as a lamb for the slaughter" (1 Pet. 1:19, 20). When I have considered also the truth of his resurrection, and have remembered that word, "Touch me not, Mary," etc., I have seen, as if he had leaped out of the grave's mouth for joy, that he was risen again and had got the conquest over our dreadful foes! (John 20:17). I have also in the spirit seen him a man, on the right hand of God the Father for me; and have seen the manner of his coming from heaven, to judge the world with glory, and have been confirmed in these things by these Sciptures following: Acts 1:9, 10; 7:56; 10:42; Heb. 7:24; 8:1; Rev. 1:18; 1 Thess. 4:17, 18.

Once I was troubled to know whether the Lord Jesus was man as well as God, and God as well as man; and truly, in those days, let men say what they would, unless I had it with evidence from heaven, all was nothing to me.

Well, I was much troubled about this point, and could not tell how to be resolved; at last, that in Rev. 5 came into my mind, "And I beheld, and lo, in the midst of the throne, and of the four beasts, and in the midst of the elders, stood a Lamb." In the midst of the throne, thought I, there is the Godhead; in the midst of the elders, there is the Manhood. But oh! methought this did glister! It was a goodly touch, and gave me sweet satisfaction. That other scripture did also help me much in this: "Unto us a child is born, unto us a son is given, and the government shall be upon his shoulder; and his name shall be called Wonderful, Counsellor, the Mighty God, the Everlasting Father, the Prince of Peace," etc. (Isa. 9:6).

Also, besides these teachings of God in his word, the Lord made use of two things to confirm me in his truth: the one was the errors of the Quakers, and the other was the guilt of sin. For as the Quakers did oppose the truth, so God did the more confirm me in it by leading me into the Scriptures that did wonderfully maintain it. . . .

And as I said, the guilt of sin did help me much; for still as that would come upon me, the blood of Christ did take it off again and again and again, and that too, sweetly, according to the Scripture. O friends! cry to

God to reveal Jesus Christ unto you; there is none teacheth like him.

It would be too long here to say, to tell you in particular how God did set me down in all the things of Christ; yea, and also how he did open his words unto me, and make them shine before me, and cause them to dwell with me, talk with me, and comfort me over and over, both of his own being, and the being of his Son, and Spirit, and Word, and gospel. Only this, as I said before, I will say unto you again, that in general he was pleased to take this course with me, first to suffer me to be afflicted with temptations concerning them, and then reveal them to me. As sometimes I would lie under great guilt for sin, even crusht to the ground therewith; and then the Lord would show me the death of Christ; yea, so sprinkle my conscience with his blood, that I should find, and that before I was aware, that in that conscience, where but just now did reign and rage the law, even there would rest and abide the peace and love of God through Christ.

Now I had an evidence, as I thought, of my salvation, from heaven, with many golden seals thereon, all hanging in my sight. Now could I remember this manifestation, and the other discovery of grace with comfort; and would often long and desire that the last day were come, that I might be for ever inflamed with the sight, and joy, and communion with him whose head was crowned with thorns, whose face was spit upon, and body broken, and soul made an offering for my sins. For whereas before I lay continually trembling at the mouth of hell, now methought I was got so far therefrom that I could, when I looked back, scarce discern it. And oh! thought I, that I were fourscore years old now, that I might die quickly, that my soul might be gone to rest!

But before I had got thus far out of these my temptations, I did greatly long to see some ancient godly man's experience, who had lived some hundreds of years before I was born. Well, after many such longings in my mind, the God in whose hands are all our days and ways did cast into my hand, one day, a book of Martin Luther's. It was his comment on the Galatians; it also was so old, that it was ready to fall piece by piece, if I did but turn it over. Now I was pleased much that such an old book had fallen into my hands; which, when I had but a little way perused, I found my condition in his experience so largely and profoundly handled as if his book had been written out of my heart. This made me marvel; for thus thought I, this man could not know any thing of the state of Christians now, but must needs write and speak the experience of former days. Besides, he doth most gravely also in that book debate of the rise of these temptations, namely, blasphemy, desperation, and the like; showing that the law of Moses, as well as the devil, death, and hell, hath a very great hand therein: which, at first, was very strange to me; but considering and watching, I found it so indeed. But of particulars here, I intend nothing; only that I do prefer this book of Martin Luther's upon the Galatians (excepting the Holy Bible) before all the books that ever I have seen as most fit for a wounded conscience.

And now I found, as I thought, that I loved Christ dearly. Oh! methought my soul cleaved unto him, my affections cleaved unto him. I felt my love to him as hot as fire. But I did quickly find that my great love was but too little; and that I, who had, as I thought, such burning love to Jesus Christ, could let him go again for a trifle. God can tell how to abase us, and can hide pride from man. Quickly after this, my love was tried to the purpose.

The Great Trial of His Love to Christ

1652-1653

For, after the Lord had in this manner thus graciously delivered me from this great and sore temptation, and had given me such strong consolation and blessed evidence from heaven touching my interest in his love through Christ, the tempter came upon me again, and that with more grievous and dreadful temptation than before. And that was, to sell and part with the most blessed Christ, to exchange him for the things of this life—for any thing. The temptation lay upon me for the space of a year, and did follow me so continually, that I was not rid of it one day in a month; no, not sometimes one hour in many days together, unless when I was asleep.

And tho, in my judgment, I was persuaded that those who were once effectually in Christ (as I hoped, through his grace, I had seen myself) could never lose him for ever ("For the land shall not be sold for ever, for the land is mine," saith God; Lev. 25:23), yet it was a continual vexation to me to think that I should have so much as one such thought within me against a Christ, a Jesus, that had done for me as he had done; and yet then I had almost none others but such blasphemous ones.

But it was neither by dislike of the thought, nor yet any desire and endeavor to resist it, that in the least did shake or abate the continuation or force and strength thereof. For it did always, in almost whatever I thought, intermix itself therewith in such sort that I could neither eat my food, stoop for a pin, chop a stick, or cast mine eye to look on this or that, but still the temptation would come, "Sell Christ for this! or sell Christ for that! sell him! sell him!" Sometimes it would run in my thoughts, not so little as a hundred times together, "Sell him! sell him!" against which I may say for whole hours together I have been forced to stand as continually leaning and forcing my spirit against it, lest haply, before I were aware, some wicked thought might arise in my heart, that I might consent thereto. Sometimes indeed the tempter would make me believe I had consented to it; and then I would be as tortured upon a rack for whole days together.

This temptation did put me to such scares lest I should at sometimes, I say, consent thereto, and be overcome therewith, that by the very force of my mind my very body would be put into action or motion, by way of pushing or thrusting with my hands or elbows; still answering, as fast as the destroyer said, "Sell him," "I will not, I will not, I will not; no, not for thousands, thousands, thousands of worlds" (thus reckoning, lest I should set too low a value on him): even until I scarce well knew where I was or how to be composed again. At these seasons he would not let me eat any food at quiet. But forsooth, when I was set at the table at any meat, I must go hence to pray; I must leave my food now, and just now; so counterfeit holy also would this devil be! When I was thus tempted, I would say in myself, now I am at meat, let me make an end. "No," said he, "you must do it now, or you will displease God, and despise Christ." Wherefore I was much afflicted with these things. For if because of the sinfulness of my nature (imagining that these were impulses from God) I should deny to do it, I shall feel as if I denied God; and then should I be as guilty because I did not obey a temptation of the devil, as if I had broken the law of God indeed.

But to be brief. One morning as I did lie in my bed, I was as at other times most fiercely assaulted with this temptation to sell and part with Christ; the wicked suggestion still running in my mind, "Sell him, sell him, sell him, sell him!" as fast as a man could speak; against which also in my mind, as at other times, I answered, "No, no, not for thousands, thousands, thousands!" at least twenty times together. But at last, after much striving, even till I was almost out of breath, I felt this thought pass through my heart, "Let him go, if he will"; and I thought also, that I felt my heart freely consent thereto. Oh! the diligence of Satan! Oh! the desperateness of man's heart.

Now was the battle won, and down fell I, as a bird that is shot from the top of a tree, into great guilt and fearful despair. Thus, getting out of my bed, I went moping into the field; but, God knows, with as heavy a heart as mortal man, I think, could bear; where, for the space of two hours, I was like a man bereft of life; as now past all recovery, and bound over to eternal punishment.

And withal, that scripture did seize upon my soul: "Or profane person, as Esau, who, for one morsel of meat, sold his birthright: for ye know how that afterward, when he would have inherited the blessing, he was rejected; for he found no place of repentance, though he sought it carefully with tears" (Heb. 12:16, 17). Now was I as one bound. I felt myself shut up unto the judgment to come. Nothing now, for two years together, would abide with me but damnation and an expectation of damnation. I say, nothing now would abide with me but this, save some few moments for relief, as in the sequel you will see. These words were to my soul like fetters of brass to my legs, in the continual sound of which I went for several months together.

But about ten or eleven o'clock on that day, as I was walking under a hedge (full of sorrow and guilt, God knows), and bemoaning myself for this hard hap that such a thought should arise within me, suddenly this sentence rushed in upon me, The blood of Christ remits all guilt. At this I made a stand in my spirit. With that, this word took hold upon me, "The blood of Jesus Christ, his own Son, cleanseth us from all sin" (1 John 1:7). Now I began to conceive peace in my soul; and methought I saw as if the tempter did leer and steal away from me, as being ashamed of what he had done. At the same time also I had my sin and the blood of Christ thus represented to me—that my sins when compared to the blood of Christ was no more to it than this little clod or stone before me is to this vast and wide field that here I see. This gave me good encouragement for the space of two or three hours; in which time also methought I saw, by faith, the Son of God as suffering for my sins. But because it tarried not, I therefore sunk in my spirit, under exceeding guilt again. But chiefly by the aforementioned scripture concerning Esau's selling his birthright; for that scripture would lie all day long in my mind, and hold me down, so that I could by no means lift up myself. For when I would strive to turn to this scripture or that for relief, still that sentence would be sounding in me—"For ye know how that afterward, when he would have inherited the blessing, he found no place of repentance, tho he sought it carefully with tears." Sometimes, indeed, I would have a touch from that in Luke 22:32: "I have prayed for thee that thy faith fail not"; but it would not abide upon me. Neither could I indeed, when I considered my state, find ground to conceive in the least that there should be the root of that grace in me, having sinned as I had done. Now was I torn and rent in a heavy case for many days together.

Then began I, with sad and careful heart, to consider the nature and largeness of my sin, and to search into the word of God, if I could in any place espy a word of promise, by which I might take relief. Wherefore I began to consider that of Mark 3:28: "All manner of sins and blasphemies shall be forgiven unto the sons of men, wherewith soever they shall blaspheme." Which place, methought, at a blush, did contain a large and glorious promise for the pardon of high offenses; but considering the place more fully, I thought it was rather to be understood as relating more chiefly to those who had, while in a natural state, committed such things as there are mentioned; but not to me, who had not only received light and mercy, but that had, both after and also contrary to that, so slighted Christ as I had done. I feared therefore that this wicked sin of mine might be that sin unpardonable, of which he there thus speaketh: "But he that shall blaspheme against the Holy Ghost, hath never forgiveness, but is in danger of eternal damnation" (Mark 3:29). And I did the rather give credit to this, because of that sentence in the Hebrews: "For ye know how that afterward, when he would have inherited the blessing, he was rejected: for he found no place of repentance, though he sought it carefully with tears." And this stuck always with me.

And now I was both a burden and a terror to myself; now was I weary of my life, and yet afraid to die. Oh! how gladly now would I have been anybody but myself! anything but a man! and in any condition but my own! For there was nothing did pass more frequently over my mind than it was impossible for me to be forgiven my trangression, and to be saved from the wrath to come.

And now I began to call back time that was past; wishing a thousand times twice told that the day was yet to come when I should be tempted to such a sin; concluding with great indignation, both against my heart and all assaults, how I would rather have been torn in pieces than be found a consenter thereto! But, alas! these wishings and resolvings were now too late to help me; this thought had passed my heart. God hath let me go, and I am fallen. "Oh!" thought I, "that it was with me as in months past, as in the days when God preserved me!" (Job 29:2).

Then again, being loath and unwilling to perish, I began to compare my sin with others, to see if I could find any of those who were saved had done as I had done. So I considered David's adultery and murder, and found them most heinous crimes; and those too committed after light and grace received. But yet, by considering, I perceive that his transgressions were only such as were against the law of Moses, from which the Lord Christ could, with the consent of his word, deliver him: but mine was against the gospel, yea, against the Mediator thereof; I had sold my Savior! Now again would I be racked upon the wheel, when I considered that, besides the guilt that possest me, I should be so void of grace, so bewitched! What, thought I, must it be no sin but this? Must it needs be "the great transgression?" (Ps. 19:13). Must that wicked one touch my soul? (1 John 5:18). Oh! what sting did I find in all these sentences! "What (thought I), is there but one sin that is unpardonable? But one sin that layeth the soul without the reach of God's mercy; and must I be guilty of that? Is there but one sin among so many millions of sins for which there is no forgiveness, and must I commit this! Oh! unhappy sin! Oh! unhappy man!" These things would so break and confound my spirit that I thought at times they would have broke my wits; and still to aggravate my misery that would run in my mind, "Ye know how, that afterward when he would have inherited the blessing, he was rejected." Oh! no one knows the terror of those days but myself.

After this I began to consider Peter's sin, which he committed in denying his Master. And indeed, this came nighest to mine of any that I could find; for he had denied his Savior, as I, after light and mercy received; yea, and that too, after warning given him. I also considered that he did it once and twice: and that, after time to consider betwixt. But tho I put all these circumstances together, that, if possible, I might find help, yet I considered again that his was but a denial of his Master, but mine was a selling of my Savior. Wherefore I thought with myself that I came nearer to Judas, than either to David or Peter. Here again my torment would flame out and afflict me; yea, it would grind me, as it were, to powder, to consider the preservation of God toward others while I fell into the snare; for I could evidently see God preserved them, notwithstanding their wickedness, and would not let them, as he had let me, become a son of perdition.

But oh! how did my soul at this time, prize the preservation that God did set about his people! Ah, how safely did I see them walk whom God had hedged in! They were within his care, protection, and special providence; tho they were full as bad as I by nature, yet, because he loved them, he would not suffer them to fall without the range of mercy: but as for me, he would not preserve me nor keep me; but suffered me, because I was a reprobate, to fall as I had done! Now did those blessed places that speak of God's keeping his people, shine like the sun before me, tho not to comfort me, yet to show me the blessed state and heritage of those whom the Lord hath blest. Now I saw that as God had his hand in all the providences and dispensations that overtook his elect, so he had his hand in all the temptations that they had to sin against him; not to animate them to wickedness, but to choose their temptations and troubles for them, and also to leave them for a time to such things only that might not destroy, but humble them; as might not put them beyond, but lay them in the way of the renewing of his mercy. But oh! what love, what care, what kindness and mercy did I now see, mixing itself with the most severe and dreadful of all God's ways to his people! He would let David, Hezekiah, Solomon, Peter, and others fall, but he would not let them fall into the sin unpardonable, nor into hell for sin. "O! thought I, these be the men that God hath loved; these be the men that God, tho he chastiseth them, keeps them in safety by him." But all these thoughts added sorrow, grief, and horror to me; as whatever I now thought on, it was killing to me. If I thought how God kept his own, that was killing to me; if I thought of how I was fallen myself, that was killing to me. As all things wrought together for the best, and to do good to them that were the called, according to his purpose; so I thought all things wrought together for my damage and for my eternal overthrow.

Then again I began to compare my sin with the sin of Judas, that, if possible, I might find if mine differed from that, which in truth is unpardonable. And oh! thought I, if it should differ but the breadth of a hair, what a happy condition is my soul in! And by considering, I found that Judas did this intentionally, but mine was against my prayer and strivings; besides, his was committed with much deliberation, but mine in a fearful hurry, on a sudden. All this while I was tossed to and fro like the locust and driven from trouble to sorrow; hearing always the sound of Esau's fall in mine ears, and the dreadful consequences thereof. Yet this consideration about Judas' sin was, for a while, some little relief to me; for I saw I had not, as to the circumstances, transgressed so fully as he. But this was quickly gone again, for I thought within myself, there might be more ways than one to commit this unpardonable sin; also I thought that there might be degrees of that as well as of other transgressions; wherefore, for aught I could yet perceive, this iniquity of mine might be such as might never be passed by. I was often now ashamed that I should be like such an ugly man as Judas. I thought also how loathsome I should be unto all the saints in the day of judgment. Insomuch, that now I scarce could see a good man, that I believed had a good conscience, but I would feel my heart tremble at him while I was in his presence. Oh! now I saw a glory in walking with God, and what a mercy it was to have a good conscience before him!

I was about this time tempted to content myself by receiving some false opinions; as, that there should be no such thing as a day of judgment; that we should not rise again; and that sin was no such grievous thing; the tempter suggesting thus: "For if these things should indeed be true, yet to believe otherwise would yield you ease for the present. If you must perish, never torment yourself so much beforehand. Drive the thoughts of damning out of your mind, by possessing your mind with some such conclusions as Atheists and Ranters use to help themselves withal.'' But, oh! when such thoughts have led through my heart, how as it were within a step have death and judgment been in my view! Methought the Judge stood at the door. I was as if it was come already; so that such things could have no entertainment. But methinks I see by this that Satan will use any means to keep the soul from Christ; he loveth not an awakened frame of spirit; security, blindness, darkness, error, is the very kingdom and habitation of the wicked one.

I found it a hard work now to pray to God, because despair was swallowing me up. I thought I was as with a tempest driven away from God; for always when I cried to God for mercy, this would come in, "'Tis too late; I am lost; God hath let me fall, not to my correction, but my condemnation. My sin is unpardonable; and I know, concerning Esau, how that after he had sold his birthright, he would have inherited the blessing but was rejected.''

About this time I did light on that dreadful story of that miserable mortal Francis Spira; a book that was to my troubled spirit as salt when rubbed into a fresh wound. Every sentence in that book, every groan of that man, with all the rest of his actions in his dolors, as his tears, his prayers, his gnashing of teeth, his wringing of hands, his twisting, and languishing, and pining away under that mighty hand of God that was upon him, was as knives and daggers in my soul; especially that sentence of his was frightful to me, "Man knows the beginning of sin, but who bounds the issues thereof?" Then would the former sentence, as the conclusion of all, fall like a hot thunderbolt again upon my conscience; "For you know how that afterward, when he would have inherited the blessing, he was rejected; for he found no place of repentance, though he sought it carefully with tears." Then would I be struck into a very great trembling, insomuch that at sometimes I could, for whole days together, feel my very body, as well as my mind, to shake and totter under the sense of this dreadful judgment of God, that should fall on those that have sinned that most fearful and unpardonable sin. I felt also such a clogging and heat at my stomach, by reason of this my terror, that I was, especially at sometimes, as if my breast-bone would split asunder. Then I thought concerning that of Judas, who, by his falling headlong, burst asunder, and all his bowels gushed out (Acts 1). I feared also, that this was the mark that God did set on Cain, even continual fear and trembling under the heavy load of guilt that he had charged on him for the blood of his brother Abel. Thus did I wind, and twine, and shrink, under the burden that was upon me; which burden also did so oppress me that I could neither stand, nor go, nor lie, either at rest or quiet.

Yet that saying would sometimes come to my mind, "He hath received gifts for the rebellious" (Ps. 68:18). "The rebellious," thought I; "why, surely, they are such as once were under subjection to their prince, even those who, after they have sworn subjection to his government, have taken up arms against him. And this," thought I, "is my very condition. I once loved him, feared him, served him; but now am I a rebel. I have sold him: I have said, Let him go, if he will: but yet he has gifts for rebels, and then why not for me?" This sometimes I thought on, and would labor to take hold thereof, that some (tho small) refreshment might have been conceived by me. But in this also I missed of my desire. I was driven with force beyond it. I was like a man going to execution, even by that place where he would fain creep in and hide himself but may not.

Again, after I had thus considered the sins of the saints in particular, and found mine went beyond them, then I began to think with myself: Set the case I should put all theirs together, and mine alone against them, might I not then find encouragement? For if mine, tho bigger than any one, yet should be but equal to all, then there is hope; for that blood that hath virtue enough in it to wash away all theirs hath virtue enough in it to wash away mine, tho this one be full as big, if not bigger than theirs. Here again I would consider the sin of David, of Solomon, of Manasseh, of Peter, and the rest of the great offenders; and would also labor what I might, with fairness, to aggravate and heighten their sins by several circumstances. I would think with myself that David shed blood to cover his adultery, and that by the sword of the children of Ammon; a work that could not be done but by contrivance, which was a great aggravation to his sin. But then this would turn upon me: "Ah! but these were but sins against the law, from which there was a Jesus sent to save them; but yours is a sin against the Savior, and who shall save you from that?" Then I thought on Solomon; and how he sinned in loving strange women, in falling away to their idols, in building them temples; in doing this after light, in his old age, after great mercy received. But the same conclusion that cut me off in former consideration, cut me off as to this, namely, that all those were but sins against the law, for which God had provided a remedy. "But I had sold my Savior," and there remained no more sacrifice for sin. I would then add to these men's sins, the sins of Manasseh; how he built altars for idols in the house of the Lord; he also observed times, used enchantments, had to do with wizards, was a wizard, had his familiar spirits, burned his children in the fire in sacrifice to devils, and made the streets of Jerusalem run down with the blood of innocents. These, thought I, are great sins, sins of a bloody color; but yet it would turn again upon me: "They are none of them of the nature of yours; you have parted with Jesus; you have sold your Savior." This one consideration would always kill my heart, "My sin was point-blank against my Savior"; and that too at that height that I had in my heart said of him, "Let him go, if he will." Oh! methought this sin was bigger than the sins of a country, of a kingdom, or of a whole world. No one pardonable, nor all of them together, was able to equal mine; mine outwent them every one.

Now I would find my mind to flee from God, as from the face of a dreadful judge; yet this was my torment, I could not escape his hand. "It is a fearful thing to fall into the hands of the living God!" (Heb. 10). But blessed be his grace, that scripture, in these flying fits, would call, as running after me, "I have blotted out, as a thick cloud, thy transgressions; and as a cloud thy sins: return unto me, for I have redeemed thee'' (Isa. 44: 22). This, I say, would come in upon my mind, when I was fleeing from the face of God; for I did flee from his face, that is, my mind and spirit fled before him; by reason of his highness, I could not endure. Then would the text cry, ''Return unto me.'' It would cry aloud with a very great voice, ''Return unto me, for I have redeemed thee.'' Indeed, this would make me make a little stop, and as it were look over my shoulder behind me, to see if I could discern that the God of grace did follow me with a pardon in his hand. But I could no sooner do that but all would be clouded and darkened again by that sentence, ''For you know, how that afterward when he would have inherited the blessing, he found no place of repentance, though he sought it carefully with tears.'' Wherefore I could not refrain, but fled; tho at some times it cried, ''Return, return,'' as if it did hollow after me. But I feared to close in therewith, lest it should not come from God; for that other text, as I said, was still sounding in my conscience, ''For you know that afterward, when he would have inherited the blessing, he was rejected,'' etc.

Once, as I was walking to and fro in a good man's shop, bemoaning myself in my sad and doleful state; afflicting myself with self-abhorrence for this wicked and ungodly thought; lamenting also this hard hap of mine, that I should commit so great a sin, greatly fearing I should not be pardoned; praying also in my heart, that if this sin of mine did differ from that against the Holy Ghost, the Lord would show it me; and being now ready to sink with fear, suddenly there was, as if there had rushed in at the window, the noise of wind upon me, but very pleasant, and as if I heard a voice speaking, "Didst thou ever refuse to be justified by the blood of Christ?" And withal my whole life of profession past was in a moment opened to me; wherein I was made to see, that designedly I had not; so my heart answered groaningly, "No." Then fell, with power, that word of God upon me, "See that ye refuse not him that speaketh" (Heb. 12: 25). This made a strange seizure upon my spirit: it brought light with it, and commanded a silence in my heart of all those tumultuous thoughts that before did use, like masterless hell-hounds, to roar and bellow and make a hideous noise within me. It showed me, also, that Jesus Christ had yet a word of grace and mercy for me; that he had not, as I had feared, quite forsaken and cast off my soul. Yea, this was a kind of check for my proneness to desperation; a kind of threatening of me if I did not, notwithstanding my sins and the heinousness of them, venture my salvation upon the Son of God. But as to my determining about this strange dispensation, what it was, I know not; or from whence it came, I know not. I have not yet, in twenty years time, been able to make a judgment of it. I thought then, what here I should be loath to speak. But verily that sudden rushing wind was, as if an angel had come upon me. Both it, and the salvation, I will leave until the day of judgment: only this I say, it commanded a great calm in my soul; it persuaded me there might be hope; it showed me, as I thought, what the sin unpardonable was, and that my soul had yet the blessed privilege to flee to Jesus Christ for mercy. But I say, concerning this dispensation, I know not what yet to say of it; which was also, in truth, the cause that at first I did not speak of it in the book.[3] I do now also leave it to be thought on by men of sound judgment. I lay not the stress of my salvation thereupon, but upon the Lord Jesus, in the promise. . . .

This lasted in the savor of it for about three or four days; and then I began to mistrust, and to despair again. Wherefore still my life hung in doubts before me, not knowing which way I should go; only this I found my soul desire, even to cast itself at the foot of grace, by prayer

[3] *I.e.,* in the early editions of the present work.

and supplication. But oh! it was hard for me now to have the face to pray to this Christ for mercy, against whom I had thus vilely sinned! It was hard work, I say, to offer to look him in the face against whom I had so vilely sinned! And indeed I have found it as difficult to come to God by prayer, after backsliding from him, as to do any other thing. Oh, the shame that did now attend me! especially when I thought, "I am now going to pray to him for mercy that I have so lightly esteemed but a while before!" I was ashamed, yea, even confounded, because this villainy had been committed by me.

But I saw that there was but one way with me; I must go to him, and humble myself unto him, and beg that he, of his wonderful mercy, should show pity to me, and have mercy upon my wretched sinful soul. Which, when the tempter perceived, he strongly suggested to me that I ought not to pray to God; for prayer was not for any in my case: neither could it do me good, because I had rejected the Mediator, by whom all prayers came with acceptance to God the Father, and without whom no prayer could come into his presence: "wherefore now to pray is but to add sin to sin; yea, now to pray, seeing God has cast you off, is the next way to anger and offend him more than you ever did before. For God," saith he, "hath been weary of you for these several years already, because you are none of his: your bawling in his ears hath been no pleasant voice to him; and therefore he let you sin this sin, that you might be quite cut off; and will you pray still?" This the devil urged, and set forth that in Numbers, when Moses said to the children of Israel, That because they would not go up to possess the land, when God would have them; therefore for ever did he bar them out from thence, tho they prayed they might with tears (Num. 14:36, 37, etc.). As it is said in another place (Ex. 21:14), "The man that sins presumptuously shall be taken from God's altar, that he may die"; even as Joab was by King Solomon, when he thought to find shelter there (1 Kings 2:27, 28).

These places did pinch me very sore. Yet my case being desperate, I thought with myself, "I can but die; and if it must be so, it shall once be said that such a one died at the foot of Christ in prayer." This I did; but with great difficulty, God doth know; and that because, together with this, still that saying about Esau would be set at my heart, even like a flaming sword, to keep the way of the tree of life, lest I should take thereof and live. Oh! who knows how hard a thing I found it to come to God in prayer!

I did also desire the prayers of the people of God for me; but I feared that God would give them no heart to do it. Yea, I trembled in my soul to think that some or other of them would shortly tell me that God had said those words to them that he once did say to the prophet concerning the children of Israel, "Pray not for this people, for I have rejected them" (Jer. 11:14). So "pray not for him, for I have rejected him." Yea, I thought that he had whispered this to some of them already, only they durst not tell me so; neither durst I ask them of it for fear it should be so: it would make me quite beside myself. "Man knows the beginning of sin," said Spira; "but who bounds the issues thereof?" About this time, I took an opportunity to break my mind to an ancient Christian, and told him all my case. I told him also that I was afraid that I had sinned the sin against the Holy Ghost. And he told me he thought so too. Here, therefore, I had but cold comfort; but talking a little more with him, I found him, tho a good man, a stranger to much combat with the devil. Wherefore I went to God again, as well as I could, for mercy still.

Now also did the tempter begin to mock me in my misery, saying, That seeing I had thus parted with the Lord Jesus, and provoked him to displeasure who would have stood between my soul and the flames of devouring fire, there was now but one way, and that was, to pray that God the Father would be a mediator betwixt his Son and me, that we might be reconciled again, and that I might have that blessed benefit in him that his blessed saints enjoyed. Then did that scripture seize upon my soul, "He is of one mind, and who can turn him?" Oh! I saw it was as easy to persuade him to make a new world, a new covenant, or a new Bible besides that we have already, as to pray for such a thing. This was to persuade him that what he had done already was mere folly; and persuade him to alter, yea, to disannul, the whole way of salvation. And then would that saying rend my soul asunder, "Neither is there salvation in any other; for there is none other name under heaven given among men, whereby we must be saved" (Acts 4: 12).

Now the most free and full and gracious words of the gospel were the greatest torments to me; yea, nothing so afflicted me as the thoughts of Jesus Christ. The remembrance of a Savior, because I had cast him off, brought forth the villainy of my sin and my loss by it to mind; nothing did twinge my conscience like this. Every thing that I thought of the Lord Jesus, of his grace, love, goodness, kindness, gentleness, meekness, death, blood, promises, and blessed exhortations comforts, and consolations, went to my soul like a sword. For still unto these my considerations of the Lord Jesus these thoughts would make place for themselves in my heart. "Ay, this is the Jesus, the loving Savior, the Son of God, whom you have parted with, whom you have slighted, despised and abused! This is the only Savior, the only Redeemer, the only one that could so love sinners as to wash them from their sins in his own most precious blood; but you have no part nor lot in this Jesus; you have put him from you, you have said in your heart, 'Let him go, if he will!' Now therefore you are severed from him; you have severed yourself from him. Behold then his goodness, but yourself to be no partaker of it." Oh, thought I, what have I lost! what have I parted with! what has disinherited my poor soul! Oh! it is sad to be destroyed by the grace and mercy of God; to have the Lamb, the Savior, turn lion and destroyer (Rev. 5). I also trembled, as I have said, at the sight of the saints of God, especially at those that greatly loved him, and that made it their business to walk continually with him in this world; for they did, both in their words, their carriages, and all their expressions of tenderness and fear to sin against their precious Savior, condemn, lay guilt upon, and also add continued affliction and shame unto my soul. The dread of them was put upon me, and I trembled at God's Samuels (1 Sam. 16:4).

Now also the tempter began afresh to mock my soul another way, saying that "Christ indeed did pity my case, and was sorry for my loss; but forasmuch as I had sinned and transgrest, as I had done, he could by no means help me, nor save me from what I feared. For my sin was not of the nature of theirs for whom he had bled and died; neither was it counted with those that were laid to his charge when he hanged on a tree; therefore, unless he should come down from heaven and die anew for this sin, tho indeed he did greatly pity me, yet I could have no benefit of him."

These things may seem ridiculous to others, even as ridiculous as they were in themselves; but to me they were most tormenting cogitations; every one of them augmented my misery, that Jesus Christ should have so much love as to pity me when yet he could not help me. Nor did I think, that the reason why he could not help me was because his merits were weak or his grace and salvation spent on others already: but because his faithfulness to his threatenings would not let him extend his mercy to me. Besides, I thought, as I have already hinted, that my sin was not within the bounds of that pardon that was wrapt up in a promise; and if not, then I knew surely that it was more easy for heaven and earth to pass away than for me to have eternal life. So that the ground of all these fears of mine did arise from a stedfast belief that I had of the stability of the holy Word of God, and also from my being misinformed of the nature of my sin. But oh! how this would add to my affliction, to conceit that I should be guilty of such a sin for which he did not die! These thoughts did so confound me, and imprison me, and tie me up from faith, that I knew not what to do. But oh! thought I, that he would come down again! Oh, that the work of man's redemption was yet to be done by Christ! How would I pray him, and entreat him, to count and reckon this sin among the rest for which he died! But this scripture would strike me down as dead, "Christ being raised from the dead, dieth no more; death hath no more dominion over him" (Rom. 6:9).

Thus, by the strange and unusual assaults of the tempter, was my soul like a broken vessel, driven as with the winds, and tossed sometimes headlong into despair, sometimes upon the covenant of works, and sometimes to wish that the new covenant, and the conditions thereof, might, so far forth as I thought myself concerned, be turned another way and changed. But in all these I was as those that jostle against the rocks—more broken, scattered, and rent. Oh! the unthought-of imaginations, frights, fears, and terrors, that are effected by a thorough application of guilt, yielding to desperation! This is the man that hath his dwelling among the tombs with the dead; that is always crying out, and cutting himself with stones (Mark 5:1-3). But, I say, all in vain! Desperation will not comfort him; the old covenant will not save him: nay, heaven and earth shall pass away, before one jot or tittle of the word and law of grace will fail or be removed. This I saw, this I felt, and under this I groaned. Yet this advantage I got thereby, namely, a farther confirmation of the certainty of the way of salvation, and that the Scriptures were the Word of God. Oh! I can not now express what then I saw and felt, of the steadiness of Jesus Christ, the rock of man's salvation. What was done could not be undone, added to, nor altered. I saw, indeed, that sin might drive the soul beyond Christ, even the sin which is unpardonable; but wo to him that was so driven, for the Word would shut him out!

Thus was I always sinking, whatever I did think or do. So one day I walked to a neighboring town, and sat down upon a settle in the street, and fell into a very deep pause about the most fearful state my sin had brought me to. And after long musing, I lifted up my head; but methought I saw as if the sun that shineth in the heavens did grudge to give light; and as if the very stones in the street and tiles upon the houses did bend themselves against me! Methought that they all combined together, to banish me out of the world! I was abhorred of them, and unfit to dwell among them, or be partaker of their benefits, because I had sinned against the Savior. O how happy now was every creature over what I was! for they stood fast and kept their station, but I was gone and lost! Then, breaking out in the bitterness of my soul, I said to my soul with a grievous sigh, "How can God comfort such a wretch as I am?" I had no sooner said it, but this returned upon me, as an echo doth answer a voice, "This sin is not unto death." At which I was as if I had been raised out of the grave, and cried out again, "Lord, how couldst thou find out such a word as this!" For I was filled with admiration at the fitness and at the unexpectedness of the sentence. The fitness of the word; the rightness of the timing of it; the power, and sweetness, and light, and glory that came with it also were marvelous to me to find. I was now, for the time, out of doubt as to that about which I was so much in doubt before. My fears before were that my sin was not pardonable, and so that I had no right to pray, to repent, etc., or that if I did, it would be of no advantage to me. But now, thought I, if this sin is not unto death, then it is pardonable; therefore from this I have encouragement to come to God by Christ for mercy; to consider the promise of forgiveness as that which stands with open arms to receive me as well as others. This therefore was a great easement to my mind, namely, that my sin was pardonable, that is, was not the sin unto death (1 John 5:16, 17). None but those that know by their own experience what my trouble was can tell what relief came to my soul by this consideration. It was a release to me from my former bonds and a shelter from my former storms. I seemed now to stand upon the same ground with other sinners, and to have as good right to the word and prayer as any of them.

Now, I say, I was in hopes that my sin was not unpardonable, but that there might be hopes for me to obtain forgiveness. But, oh, how Satan did now lay about him, to bring me down again! But he could by no means do it, neither this day nor the most part of the next; for this sentence stood like a mill-post at my back. Yet toward the evening of the next day I felt this word begin to leave me and to withdraw its support from me; and so I returned to my old fears again: but with a great deal of grudging and peevishness, for I feared the sorrow of despair; nor could my faith now long retain this word.

But the next day at evening, being under many fears, I went to seek the Lord; and as I prayed I cried, and my soul cried to him in these words, with strong cries: "O Lord, I beseech thee, show me that thou hast loved me with everlasting love" (Jer. 31:3). I had no sooner said it, but with sweetness this returned upon me, as an echo, or sounding again, "I have loved thee with an everlasting love." Now I went to bed in quiet; also when I waked the next morning, it was fresh upon my soul, and I believed it. But yet the tempter left me not; for it could not be so little as a hundred times that he, that day, did labor to break my peace. Oh! the comforts and conflicts that I did then meet with as I strove to hold by this word! That of Esau would fly in my face like lightning. I would be sometimes up and down twenty times in an hour. Yet God did bear me out, and keep my heart upon this word; from which I had also for several days together very much sweetness and comfortable hopes of pardon; for thus it was made out unto me, "I loved thee whilst thou wast committing this sin; I loved thee before; I love thee still, and I will love thee for ever."

Yet I saw my sin most barbarous and a filthy crime, and could not but conclude with great shame and astonishment that I had horribly abused the holy Son of God. Wherefore I felt my soul greatly to love and pity him, and my bowels to yearn toward him; for I saw he was still my Friend, and did reward me good for evil. Yea, the love and affection that then did burn within to my Lord and Savior Jesus Christ did work at this time such a strong and hot desire of revengement upon myself for the abuse I had done unto him, that, to speak as I then thought, had I a thousand gallons of blood within my veins, I could freely then have spilt it all at the command and feet of this my Lord and Savior.

And as I was thus musing, and in my studies considering how to love the Lord and to express my love to him, that saying came in upon me, "If thou, Lord, shouldst mark iniquity, O Lord, who should stand? But there is forgiveness with thee, that thou mayst be feared" (Ps. 130:4). These were good words to me, especially the latter part thereof, namely, that there is forgiveness with the Lord, that he might be feared; that is, as I then understood it, that he might be loved and had in reverence. For it was thus made out to me, That the great God did set so high an esteem upon the love of his poor creatures that, rather than he would go without their love, he would pardon their transgression. And now was that word fulfilled on me, and I was also refreshed by it, "Then shall they be ashamed and confounded, and never open their mouth any more because of their shame, when I am pacified toward them for all that they had done, saith the Lord God" (Ezek. 16:63). Thus was my soul at this time, and as I then did think for ever, set at liberty from being afflicted with my former guilt and amazement.

But before many weeks were gone, I began to despond again, fearing, lest notwithstanding all that I had enjoyed, that I might be deceived and destroyed at the last. For this consideration came strong into my mind, That whatever comfort and peace I thought I might have from the word of the promise of life, yet unless there could be found in my refreshment, a concurrence and agreement in the Scriptures, let me think what I will thereof and hold it never so fast, I should find no such thing at the end; for the Scriptures can not be broken (John 10:35). Now began my heart again to ache and fear I might meet with a disappointment at last. Wherefore I began with all seriousness to examine my former comfort, and to consider whether one that had sinned as I had done might with confidence trust upon the faithfulness of God laid down in these words by which I had been comforted, and on which I had leaned myself. But now were brought to my mind the words: "For it is impossible for those who were once enlightened, and have tasted the heavenly gift, and were made partakers of the Holy Ghost, and have tasted the good word of God, and the powers of the world to come, if they shall fall away, to renew them again unto repentance" (Heb. 6). "For if we sin wilfully after we have received the knowledge of the truth, there remains no more sacrifice for sin; but a certain fearful looking for of judgment, and fiery indignation, which shall devour the adversaries" (Heb. 10). "Even as Esau, who for one morsel of meat, sold his birthright. For you know how that afterward, when he would have inherited the blessing, he was rejected; for he found no place of repentance, though he sought it carefully with tears" (Heb. 12). Now was the word of the gospel forced from my soul; so that no promise or encouragement was to be found in the Bible for me. And now would that saying work upon my spirit to afflict me, "Rejoice not, O Israel, for joy, as other people" (Hos. 9:1). For I saw indeed there was cause of rejoicing for those that held to Jesus; but as for me, I had cut myself off by my transgressions, and left myself neither foot-hold, nor hand-hold, among all the stays and props in the precious word of life. And truly I did now feel myself to sink into a gulf, as a house whose foundation is destroyed. I did liken myself in this condition unto the case of a child that was fallen into a mill-pit, who tho it could make some shift to scrabble and sprawl in the water, yet because it could find neither hold for hand nor foot, therefore at last it must die in that condition.

So soon as this fresh assault had fastened on my soul, that scripture came into my heart, "This is for many days" (Dan. 10:14). And indeed I found it was so; for I could not be delivered, nor brought to peace again, until well nigh two years and a half were completely finished. Wherefore these words, tho in themselves they tended to discouragement, yet to me, who feared this condition would be eternal, they were at sometimes as a help and refreshment to me. For, thought I, many days are not for ever; many days will have an end; therefore seeing I was to be afflicted not a few, but many days, yet I was glad it was but for many days. Thus, I say, I could recall myself sometimes, and give myself a help; for as soon as ever the words came into my mind at first, I knew my trouble would be long. Yet this would be but sometimes; for

I could not always think on this, nor ever be helped by it tho I did.

Now, while these scriptures lay before me, and laid sin anew at my door, that saying in Luke 18:1, with others, did encourage me to prayer. Then the tempter again laid at me very sore, suggesting that neither the mercy of God nor yet the blood of Christ did at all concern me, nor could they help me for my sin; therefore it was but in vain to pray. Yet, thought I, "I will pray." "But," said the tempter, "your sin is unpardonable." "Well," said I, "I will pray." "'Tis to no boot," said he. "Yet," said I, "I will pray." So I went to pray to God; and while I was at prayer, I uttered words to this effect: "Lord, Satan tells me, that neither thy mercy, nor Christ's blood, is sufficient to save my soul: Lord, shall I honor thee most, by believing thou wilt and canst? or him, by believing thou neither wilt nor canst? Lord I would fain honor thee, by believing thou wilt and canst." And as I was thus before the Lord, that scripture fastened on my heart, "O man, great is thy faith!" (Matt. 15:28) even as if one had clapped me on the back, as I was on my knees before God. Yet I was not able to believe this, that this was a prayer of faith, till almost six months after; for I could not think that I had faith, or that there should be a word for me to act faith on. Therefore I would still be as sticking in the jaws of desperation, and went mourning up and down in a sad condition.

There was nothing now that I longed for more than to be put out of doubt as to this thing in question; and as I was vehemently desiring to know if there was indeed hope for me, these words came rolling into my mind: "Will the Lord cast off for ever? and will he be favorable no more? Is his mercy clean gone for ever? doth his promise fail for evermore? Hath God forgotten to be gracious? hath he in anger shut up his tender mercies?" (Ps. 77:7, 8, 9). And all the while they run in my mind, methought I had still this as the answer: "'Tis a question whether he hath or no; it may be he hath not." Yea, the interrogatory seemed to me to carry in it a sure affirmation, that indeed he had not, nor would so cast off, but would be favorable; that his promise doth not fail; and that he hath not forgotten to be gracious, nor would in anger shut up his tender mercy. Something also there was upon my heart at the same time, which I now can not call to mind, which with this text did sweeten my heart and made me conclude that his mercy might not be quite gone, nor gone for ever.

At another time I remember I was again

much under this question, "Whether the blood of Christ was sufficient to save my soul?" In which doubt I continued from morning till about seven or eight at night; and at last, when I was, as it were, quite worn out with fear lest it should not hold on me, these words did sound suddenly within my heart, "He is able." But methought this word able was spoke loud unto me; it showed a great word; it seemed to be writ in great letters; and gave such a justle to my fear and doubt (I mean for the time it tarried with me, which was about a day) as I never had from that all my life, either before or after (Heb. 7:25).

But one morning as I was again at prayer, and trembling under the fear of this, that no word of God could help me, that piece of a sentence darted in upon me, "My grace is sufficient." At this methought I felt some stay, as if there might be hopes. But oh! how good a thing it is for God to send his word! For about a fortnight before I was looking on this very place, and then I thought it could not come near my soul with comfort; therefore I threw down my book in a pet. Then I thought it was not large enough for me; no, not large enough! But now it was as if it had arms of grace so wide that it could not only inclose me, but many more besides. By these words I was sustained, yet not without exceeding conflicts, for the space of seven or eight weeks: for my peace would be in it and out sometimes twenty times a day; comfort now, and trouble presently; peace now, and before I could go a furlong, as full of fear and guilt as ever heart could hold; and this was not only now and then, but my whole seven weeks' experience. For this about the sufficiency of grace and that of Esau's parting with his birthright would be like a pair of scales within my mind; sometimes one end would be uppermost, and sometimes again the other; according to which would be my peace or trouble. Therefore I did still pray to God, that he would come in with this scripture more fully on my heart, that is, that he would help me to apply the whole sentence. For as yet I could not; that he gave, that I gathered; but farther I could not go; for as yet it only helped me to hope that there might be mercy for me. "My grace is sufficient"; and tho it came no farther, it answered my former question, namely, that there was hope; yet because "for thee" was left out, I was not contented, but prayed to God for that also. Wherefore one day, when I was in a meeting of God's people, full of sadness and terror (for my fears again were strong upon me), and as I was now thinking my soul was never the better, but my case most sad and fearful, these words did with great power suddenly break in upon me, "My grace is sufficient for thee! My grace is sufficient for thee! My grace is sufficient for thee!" three times together. And, oh! methought, that every word was a mighty word unto me, as my, and grace, and sufficient, for thee; they were then, and sometimes are still, far bigger than others be. At which time my understanding was so enlightened that I was as tho I had seen the Lord Jesus look down from heaven through the tiles upon me, and direct these words unto me. This sent me mourning home; it broke my heart and filled me full of joy and laid me low as the dust; only it staid not long with me, I mean in this glory and refreshing comfort; yet it continued with me for several weeks, and did encourage me to hope. But as soon as that powerful operation of it was taken from my heart, that other about Esau returned upon me as before; so my soul did hang as in a pair of scales again, sometimes up, and sometimes down, now in peace, and anon again in terror.

[There follows an account of "The Means of His Deliverance and Settled Peace" (1653), and a relation of "The Origin and Issue of the Preceding Trial, Temptations, and Trials after his Connection with the Church at Bedford," and his "Call to and Experience in the Christian Ministry."]

John Bunyan

His Blessed Experience In Bedford Jail

1660-1672

Having made profession of the glorious gospel of Christ a long time, and preached the same about five years, I was apprehended at a meeting of good people in the country; among whom, had they let me alone, I should have preached that day. But they took me away from among them, and had me before a justice; who, after I had offered security for my appearing the next sessions, yet committed me, because my sureties would not consent to be bound that I should preach no more to the people.

At the sessions after, I was indicted for an upholder and maintainer of unlawful assemblies and conventicles, and for not conforming to the national worship of the Church of England. And after some conference there with the justices, they taking up my plain dealing with them for "a confession," as they termed it, of the indictment, did sentence me to a perpetual banishment, because I refused to conform. So being again delivered up to the jailer's hands, I was had home to prison; and there have lain now complete twelve years, waiting to see what God would suffer these men to do with me. In which condition

I have continued with much content through grace; but have met with many turnings and goings upon my heart, from the Lord, from Satan, and my own corruptions. By all which, glory be to Jesus Christ, I have also received, among many things, much conviction, instruction, and understanding; of which at large I shall not here discourse, only give you a hint or two, a word that may stir up the godly to bless God and to pray for me; and also to take encouragement, should the case be their own, "not to fear what man can do unto them."

I never had in all my life so great an inlet into the word of God as now. Those scriptures that I saw nothing in before, are made in this place and state, to shine upon me. Jesus Christ also was never more real and apparent than now. Here I have seen and felt him indeed. O! that word, "We have not preached unto you cunningly devised fables" (2 Pet. 1:10), and, "God raised Christ from the dead, and gave him glory, that your faith and hope might be in God" (1 Pet. 1:21), were blessed words to me in this my present imprisoned condition. These three or four scriptures also have been great refreshments in this condition to me (John 14:1-4; 16:33; Col. 3:3, 4; Heb. 12:22-24). So that sometimes when I have been in the savor of them, I have been able "to laugh at destruction, and to fear neither the horse, nor his rider." I have had sweet sights of the forgiveness of my sins in this place, and of my being with Jesus in another world. O! the Mount Zion, the heavenly Jerusalem, the innumerable company of angels, and God the Judge of all, and the spirits of just men made perfect, and Jesus, have been sweet unto me in this place! I have seen that here that I am persuaded I shall never, while in this world, be able to express. I have seen a truth in this scripture, "Whom having not seen, ye love; in whom, though now ye see him not, yet believing, ye rejoice with joy unspeakable, and full of glory" (1 Pet. 1:8).

I never knew what it was for God to stand by me at all turns, and at every offer of Satan to afflict me, etc., as I have found him since I came in hither. For look, how fears have presented themselves, so have supports and encouragements; yea, when I have started even as it were at nothing else but my shadow, yet God, as being very tender of me, hath not suffered me to be molested, but would with one scripture or another strengthen me against all, insomuch that I have often said, "Were it lawful, I could pray for greater trouble, for the greater comfort's sake" (Eccles. 7:14; 2 Cor. 1:5).

Before I came to prison, I saw what was a coming; and had especially two considerations warm upon my heart. The first was, how to suffer patiently a long confinement; the second, how to be able to encounter death, should that be here my portion. For the first of these, that scripture, Col. 1:11, was great information to me, namely, to pray to God "to be strengthened with all might, according to his glorious power, unto all patience and long-suffering with joyfulness." I could seldom go to prayer before I was imprisoned, for not so little as a year together, but this sentence or sweet petition would, as it were, thrust itself into my mind and persuade me that if ever I would go through long-suffering, I must have patience, especially if I would endure it joyfully. As to the second consideration, that saying, 2 Cor. 1:9, was of great use to me: "But we had the sentence of death in ourselves, that we might not trust in ourselves, but in God, that raiseth the dead." By this scripture I was made to see that if ever I would suffer rightly, I must first pass a sentence of death upon every thing that can properly be called a thing of this life; even to reckon myself, my wife, my children, my health, my enjoyments, and all, as dead to me, and myself as dead to them. The second thing was, to live upon God that is invisible. As Paul said in another place, the way not to faint is "to look, not at the things that are seen, but at the things that are not seen. For the things that are seen are temporal; but the things that are not seen are eternal." And thus I reasoned with myself: "If I provide only for a prison, then the whip comes at unawares; and so doth also the pillory. Again, if I only provide for these, then I am not fit for banishment. Further, if I conclude that banishment is the worst, then if death come I am surprized. So that I see the best way to go through sufferings is to trust in God through Christ, as touching the world to come; and as touching this world, to count the grave my house, to make my bed in darkness, and to say to corruption, Thou art my father; and to the worm, Thou art my mother and sister: that is, to familiarize these things to me."

But notwithstanding these helps, I found myself a man encompassed with infirmities. The parting with my wife and poor children hath often been to me, in this place, as the pulling the flesh from my bones: and that not only because I have been somewhat too fond of these great mercies, but also because I would often have brought to my mind the many hardships, miseries, and wants, that my poor family was like to meet with; especially my poor blind child, who lay nearer my heart than all I had beside! O! the thoughts of the hardship I thought my blind one might go under would break my heart to pieces. "Poor child," thought I, "what sorrow art thou like to have for thy portion in this world! Thou must be beaten, must beg, suffer hunger, cold, nakedness, and a thousand calamities, tho I can not now endure the wind should blow upon thee." But yet recalling myself, thought I, "I must venture you all with God, tho it goeth to the quick to leave you." O! I saw in this condition I was as a man who was pulling down his house upon the head of his wife and children; yet, thought I, "I must do it; I must do it!" And now I thought on those two milch kine that were to carry the ark of God into another country, and to leave their calves behind them (1 Sam. 6:10, 11, 12).

But that which helped me in this temptation was a variety of considerations, of which three in special here I will name. The first was, the consideration of those two scriptures, "Leave thy fatherless children, I will preserve them alive, and let thy widows trust in me." And again, "The Lord said, Verily, it shall go well with thy remnant; verily, I will cause the enemy to intreat thee well in the time of evil," etc. (Jer. 49:11; 15:11).

I had also this consideration, that if I should now venture all for God, I engaged God to take care of my concernments; but if I forsook him and his ways for fear of any trouble that should come to me or mine, then I should not only falsify my profession, but should count also that my concernments were not so sure, if left at God's feet, while I stood to and for his name, as they would be if they were under my own care, tho with the denial of the way of God. This was a smarting consideration, and as spurs unto my flesh. That scripture also greatly helped it to fasten the more upon me, where Christ prays against Judas, that God would disappoint him in his selfish thoughts, which moved him to sell his Master. Pray read it soberly (Ps. 119:6-8, etc.).

I had also another consideration, and that was the dread of the torments of hell, which I was sure they must partake of that, for fear of the cross, do shrink from their profession of Christ, his words and laws, before the sons of men. I thought also of the glory that he had prepared for those that in faith and love and patience stood to his ways before them. These things, I say, have helped me, when the thoughts of the misery that both myself and mine might, for the sake of my profession, be exposed to hath lain pinching on my mind. When I have indeed conceited that I might be banished for my profession, then I have thought of that scripture, "They were stoned, they were sawn asunder, were tempted, were slain with the sword: they wandered about in sheep-skins, and goat-skins, being destitute, afflicted, tormented; of whom the world was not worthy"; for all they thought they were too bad to dwell and abide among them. I have also thought of that saying, "The Holy Ghost witnesseth in every city, that bonds and afflictions abide me." I have verily thought, that my soul and it have sometimes reasoned about the sore and sad estate of a banished and exiled condition, how they are exposed to hunger, to cold, to perils, to nakedness, to enemies, and a thousand calamities; and at last, it may be to die in a ditch, like a poor forlorn and desolate sheep. But I thank God, hitherto I have not been moved by these most delicate reasonings, but have rather, by them, more approved my heart to God.

I will tell you a pretty business. I was once above all the rest in a very sad and low condition for many weeks; at which time also I being but a young prisoner, and not acquainted with the laws, had this laid much upon my spirit—that my imprisonment might end at the gallows for aught that I could tell. Now therefore Satan laid hard at me, to beat me out of heart, by suggesting thus unto me: "But how if, when you come indeed to die, you should be in this condition, that is, as not to savor the things of God, nor to have any evidence upon your soul for a better state hereafter?" For indeed at that time all the things of God were hid from my soul. Wherefore, when I at first began to think of this, it was a great trouble to me. For I thought with myself, that in the condition I now was in I was not fit to die; neither indeed did think I could, if I should be called to it. Besides, I thought with myself, if I should make a scrambling shift to clamber up the ladder, yet I should, either with quaking, or other symptoms of fainting, give occasion to the enemy to reproach the way of God and his people for their timorousness. This therefore lay with great trouble upon me; for methought I was ashamed to die with a pale face and tottering knees in such a cause as this.

Wherefore I prayed to God, that he would comfort me, and give me strength to do and suffer what he should call me to. Yet no comfort appeared, but all continued hid. I was also at this time so really possest with the thought of death that oft I was as if on a ladder with a rope about my neck. Only this was some encouragement to me, I thought I might now have an opportunity to speak my last words unto a multitude which I thought would come to see me die; and, thought I, "if it must be so, if God will but convert one soul by my last words, I shall not count my life thrown away nor lost." But yet all the things of God were kept out of my sight, and still the tempter followed me with, "But whither must you go when you die? What will become of you? Where will you be found in another world? What evidence have you for heaven and glory, and an inheritance among them that are sanctified?" Thus was I tossed for many weeks and knew not what to do. At last this consideration fell with weight upon me, that it was for the word and way of God that I was in this condition; wherefore I was engaged not to flinch a hair's breadth from it. I thought also that God might choose whether he would give me comfort now or at the hour of death; but I might not therefore choose whether I would hold my profession or no. I was bound, but he was free: yea, 'twas my duty to stand to his word, whether he would ever look upon me or save me at the last. Wherefore, thought I, "save the point being thus, I am for going on, and venturing my eternal state with Christ, whether I have comfort here or no. If God doth not come in (thought I), I will leap off the ladder, even blindfold, into eternity; sink or swim, come heaven, come hell. Lord Jesus, if thou wilt catch me, do; if not, I will venture for thy name."

I was no sooner fixt upon this resolution, but the word dropt upon me, "Doth Job serve God for nought?" As if the accuser had said, "Lord, Job is no upright man. He serves thee for by-respects. Hast thou not made an hedge about him? etc. But put forth now thy hand, and touch all that he hath, and he will curse thee to thy face." How now, thought I, is this the sign of an upright soul, to desire to serve God, when all is taken from him? Is he a godly man that will serve God for nothing rather than give out? Blessed be God then, I hope I have an upright heart; for I am resolved (God giving me strength) never to deny my profession, tho I have nothing at all for my pains. And as I was thus considering, that scripture was set before me, Ps. 44:12, etc. Now was my heart full of comfort, for I hoped it was sincere. I would not have been without this trial for much. I am comforted every time I think of it; and I hope I shall bless God for ever, for the teaching I have had by it. Many more of the dealings of God toward me, I might relate. "But these out of the spoils won in battle have I dedicated to maintain the house of God" (1 Chron. 26:27).

A Prayer of Franz Volkmar Reinhard

Accomplish thy perfect work in our souls, O Father; let us become day by day purer, freer, more heavenly, more happy, and preserve us unto eternal life. Bless, animate, and sustain us, and raise us mightily, above all that would distract us, to thyself and the consciousness of thy fellowship, which gives joy to all who dwell therein. As yet we are bound with many chains; we tarry among things seen and temporal, and feel their oppression; we are exposed to the storms of the outer world, and are wrestling with its ills. But we are not dismayed, for we are more than earth and dust, we are akin to thee, O Spirit of the Lord, and can experience thy heavenly influence. Unite us evermore closely to the company of faithful hearts whom thou art sanctifying and preparing for heaven; fill us with their faith and love and hope. AMEN.

SELECTIONS FROM

A Saint Indeed, or the Great Work of a Christian In Keeping the Heart In the Several Conditions of Life

BY

JOHN FLAVEL

JOHN FLAVEL

English Nonconformist divine, was born at Bromsgrove, Worcestershire, c. 1630; died at Exeter, Devonshire, June 26, 1691. He was educated at University College, Oxford, took Presbyterian orders (1650), and had already held livings at Diptford (in Devon) and Dartmouth, when he was ejected by the Act of Uniformity of 1662. He continued to preach privately at Dartmouth, and after the Declaration of Indulgence (1687) was minister of a Nonconformist church there. Flavel was a voluminous writer of popular works strongly evangelical in sentiment, including "Husbandry Spiritualized" (London, 1669); "Navigation Spiritualized" (1671); "A Saint Indeed or the Great Work of a Christian in Keeping the Heart" (1671); "The Fountain of Life Opened" (1672); "The Seaman's Companion" (1676); and "An Exposition of the Assembly's Catechism" (1693).

What It Is to Keep the Heart

[Keep thy heart with all diligence, for out of it are the issues of life.—Prov. 4 : 23.]

The heart of man is his worst part before it be regenerate, and the best afterward: it is the seat of principles, and fountain of actions. The eye of God is, and the eye of the Christian ought to be, principally fixt upon it.

The greatest difficulty in conversion, is, to win the heart to God; and the greatest difficulty after conversion, is, to keep the heart with God. Here lies the very pinch and stress of religion; here is that which makes the way to life a narrow way, and the gate to heaven a strait gate. Direction and help in this great work, are the scope and sum of this text; wherein we have,

I. An exhortation, "Keep thy heart with all diligence."

II. The reason, or motive enforcing it; "for out of it are the issues of life."

In the exhortation I shall consider,

1. The matter of the duty.
2. The manner of performing it.

1. The matter of the duty, "keep thy

heart." Heart is not here taken properly for that noble part of the body which philosophers call "the first that lives, and the last that dies"; but by heart, in a metaphor, the Scripture sometimes understands some particular noble faculty of the soul: in Rom. 1:21, it is put for the understanding part, their foolish heart, *i.e.*, "their foolish understanding was darkened." And Ps. 119:11, it is put for the memory: "Thy word have I hid in my heart"; and 1 John 3:10, it is put for the conscience, which hath it in both the light of the understanding, and the recognitions of the memory: if our heart condemn us, *i.e.*, if our conscience, whose proper office it is to condemn. But here we are to take it more generally for the whole soul, or inner man; for look, what the heart is to the body, that the soul is to the man; and what health is to the heart, that holiness is to the soul. The state of the whole body depends upon the soundness and vigor of the heart, and the everlasting state of the whole man upon the good or ill condition of the soul.

And by keeping the heart, understand the diligent and constant[1] use and improvement

[1] I say constant; for the reason added in the text extends the duty to all the states and conditions of a Christian's life, and makes it bind *ad semper:* if the heart must be kept because out of it are the issues of life, then as long as these issues of life do flow out of it, we are obliged to keep it.

of all holy means and duties, to preserve the soul from sin, and maintain its sweet and free communion with God. Lavater will have the word taken from a besieged garrison, begirt by many enemies without, and in danger of being betrayed by treacherous citizens within: in which danger the soldiers, upon pain of death, are commanded to watch; and whereas the expression "keep thy heart" seems to put it upon us as our work, yet it does not imply a sufficiency or ability in us to do it. We are as able to stop the sun in its course, or make the rivers run backward, as by our own skill and power to rule and order our hearts: we may as well be our own saviors, as our own keepers; and yet Solomon speaks properly enough when he says, "keep thy heart"; because the duty is ours; tho the power be God's. A natural man hath no power: a gracious man hath some, tho not sufficient; and that power he hath, depends upon the exciting and assisting strength of Christ: *gratia gratiam postulat*, grace within us is beholding to grace without us. "Without me ye can do nothing" (John 15:5). So much of the matter of the duty.

2. The manner of performing it, is "with all diligence"; the Hebrew is very emphatical, "keep with all keeping"; set double

guards, your hearts will be gone else. And this vehemency of expression with which the duty is urged plainly implies how difficult it is to keep our hearts, and how dangerous to let them go.

3. The reason or motive quickening to this duty is very forcible and weighty: "for out of it are the issues of life." That is, it is the source and fountain of all vital actions and operations; saith Jerome, "It is the spring and original both of good and evil," as the spring in a watch that sets all the wheels in motion. The heart is the treasury, the hand and tongue but the shops: what is in these, comes from thence; the hand and tongue always begin where the heart ends. The heart contrives, and the members execute. "A good man out of the good treasury of his heart bringeth forth good things, and an evil man out of the evil treasury of his heart bringeth forth evil things: for out of the abundance of his heart his mouth speaketh" (Luke 6:46). So then, if the heart err in its work, these must needs miscarry in theirs; for heart-errors are like the errors of the first concoction, which can not be rectified afterward: or like the misplacing and inverting of the stamps and letters in the press, which must needs cause so many errata in all the

copies that are printed off. O then how important a duty is that which is contained in the following proposition?

"That the keeping, and right managing of the heart in every condition, is the great business of a Christian's life."

What the philosopher saith of waters, is as properly applicable to hearts—it is hard to keep them within any bounds: God hath set bounds and limits to them, yet how frequently do they transgress not only the bounds of grace and religion, but even of reason and common honesty? This is that which affords the Christian matter of labor, fear and trembling to his dying day. It is not the cleansing of the hand that makes a Christian: for many a hypocrite can show as fair a hand as he; but the purifying, watching, and right ordering of the heart; this is the thing that provokes so many sad complaints, and costs so many deep groans and brinish tears. It was the pride of Hezekiah's heart that made him lie in the dust, mourning before the Lord (2 Chron. 32:26). It was the fear of hypocrisy invading the heart, that made David cry: "Let my heart be sound in thy statutes, that I be not ashamed" (Ps. 119:80). It was the sad experience he had of the divisions and distractions of his own heart in the service of God, that made him pour out that prayer,

"Unite my heart to fear thy name" (Ps. 86: 11).

The method in which I shall improve the point shall be this:

First, I shall inquire what the keeping of the heart supposes and imports.

Secondly, assign divers reasons, why Christians must make this the great work and business of their lives. Thirdly, point at those special seasons which especially call for this diligence in keeping the heart.

First, What the keeping of the heart supposes and imports.

To keep the heart, necessarily supposes a previous work of sanctification, which hath set the heart right, by giving it a new spiritual bent and inclination; for, as long as the heart is not set right by grace, as to its habitual frame, no duties or means can keep it right with God. Self is the poise of the unsanctified heart, which biases and moves it in all its designs and actions; and, as long as it is so, it is impossible that any external means should keep it right with God.

Man, by creation, was of one constant, uniform frame and tenor of spirit, held one straight and even course; not one thought or faculty raveled or disordered: his mind had a perfect illumination to understand and know the will of God; his will a perfect compliance therewith; his sensitive appetite, and other inferior powers, stood in a most obedient subordination.

Man, by degeneration, is become a most disordered and rebellious creature, contesting with and opposing his Maker, as the First Cause, by self-dependence; as the Chiefest Good, by self-love; as the Highest Lord, by self-will; and as the Last End, by self-seeking; and so is quite disordered, and all his acts irregular: his illuminated understanding is clouded with ignorance; his complying will, full of rebellion and stubbornness; his subordinate powers casting off the dominion and government of the superior faculties.

But by regeneration this disordered soul is set right again; sanctification being the rectifying and due framing, or, as the Scripture phrases it, "the renovation of the soul after the image of God" (Eph. 4:24), in which, self-dependence is removed by faith; self-love, by the love of God; self-will, by subjection and obedience to the will of God; and self-seeking by self-denial. The darkened understanding is again illuminated (Eph. 1:18), the refractory will sweetly subdued (Ps. 110: 3), the rebellious appetite or concupiscence gradually conquered (Rom., chaps. 6, 7). And thus the soul, which sin had universally depraved, is again by grace restored and rectified.

This being presupposed, it will not be difficult to apprehend what it is to keep the heart, which is nothing else but the constant care and diligence of such a renewed man, to preserve his soul in that holy frame to which grace hath reduced it, and daily strives to hold it.

For, tho grace hath, in a great measure, rectified the soul, and given it an habitual and heavenly temper; yet sin often actually discomposes it again; so that even a gracious heart is like a musical instrument, which, tho it be ever so exactly tuned, a small matter places out of tune again; yea, hang it aside but a little, and it will need setting again, before you can play another lesson on it: even so stands the case with gracious hearts; if they are in frame in one duty, yet how dull, dead and disordered when they come to another! And therefore every duty needs a particular preparation of the heart. "If thou prepare thine heart, and stretch out thine hands toward him" (Job. 11:13). Well then, to keep the heart, is carefully to preserve it from sin, which disorders it; and maintain that spiritual and gracious frame, which fits it for a life of communion with God. And this includes these six acts in it:

1. Frequent observation of the frame of the heart, turning in and examining how the

men pause, what is the cause of your ? Why are ye in arms?'' (Vergil).
›y is the man that thus feareth always 28:14). By this fear of the Lord it men depart from evil, shake off secur- l preserve themselves from iniquity; will keep his heart must feed with fear, with fear, and pass the whole time sojourning here in fear, and all little to keep the heart from sin.

nd lastly, to add no more, it includes lizing of God's presence with us, and the Lord always before us: thus the of God have found a singular means their hearts upright, and awe them n. When the eye of our faith is fixt ie eye of God's omniscience, we dare out our thoughts and affections to holy Job durst not suffer his heart l to an impure, vain thought; and as it that moved him to so great a pection? Why, he tells you, "doth he my ways and count all my steps?'' :4). "Walk before me'' (saith God aham) "and be thou perfect'' (Gen. Even as parents use to set their chil- the congregation before them, know- t else they will be toying and playing; d the heart of the best man too, were or the eye of God.

case stands with it; this is one part of the work: carnal and formal persons take no heed to this, they can not be brought to confer with their own hearts; there are some men and women that have lived forty or fifty years in the world, and have scarce had one hour's discourse with their own hearts all that while: it is a hard thing to bring a man and himself together upon such an account; but saints know those soliloquies and self-conferences to be of excellent use and advantage. The heathen could say, The soul is made wise by sitting still in quietness. Tho bankrupts care not to look into their books of account, yet upright hearts will know whether they go backward or forward. "I commune with mine own heart'' (Ps. 77:6). The heart can never be kept, until its case be examined and understood.

2. It includes deep humiliation for heart-evils and disorders; thus Hezekiah humbled himself for the pride of his heart (2 Chron. 32:26). Thus the people were ordered to spread forth their hands to God in prayer, in a sense of the plague of their own hearts (1 Kings 8:38). Upon this account many an upright heart had been laid low before God: O what an heart have I? They have in their confessions pointed at the heart; the pained place; Lord, here is the wound, here is the

plague-sore. It is with the heart well kept, as it is with the eye, which is a fit emblem of it, if a small dust get into the eye, it will never leave twinkling and watering till it have wept it out: so the upright heart can not be at rest till it have wept out its troubles, and poured out its complaints before the Lord.

3. It includes earnest supplications and instant prayer for heart-purifying and rectifying grace, when sin hath defiled and disordered it; so Ps. 19:12, "Cleanse thou me from secret faults"; and Ps. 86:11, "Unite my heart to fear thy name." Saints have always many such petitions depending before the throne of God's grace; this is the thing which is most pleaded by them with God: when they are praying for outward mercies, haply their spirits may be more remiss, but when it comes to the heart case, then they extend their spirits to the utmost, fill their mouths with arguments, weep and make supplication: oh, for a better heart! oh, for a heart to love God more! to hate sin more, to walk more evenly with God: Lord, deny not to me such a heart, whatever thou deny me; give me an heart to fear thee, love and delight in thee, if I beg my bread in desolate places. It is observed of holy Mr. Bradford, that when he was confessing sin, he would never give over confessing until he had felt

some brokenness of he
when praying for any s
never give over that su
relish of that mercy; t
included in keeping the

4. It includes the in
gagements and bonds u
more accurately with
occasions whereby the
to sin: well composed,
ate vows, are, in some
to guard the heart aga
so Job 31:1, "I made
eyes"; by this means,
awed their souls, and
from defilement by sc
ruptions.

5. It includes a const
our own hearts; quick-s
an excellent preservati
will keep his heart mus
soul awake and open u
and tumultuous stirrin
the affections break lo
be stirred, the soul m
press them before they
my soul, dost thou wel
tuous thoughts and pa
commission?

John Flavel

In these, and such like particulars, do gracious souls express the care they have of their hearts; they are as careful to prevent the breaking loose of their corruptions in times of temptation as seamen are to bind fast the guns, that they break not loose in a storm; as careful to preserve the sweetness and comfort they have got from God in any duty as one that comes out of an hot bath, or great sweat, is of taking cold by going forth into the chill air. This is the work, and of all works in religion it is the most difficult, constant, and important work.

1. It is the hardest work; heart-work is hard work indeed: to shuffle over religious duties with a loose and heedless spirit will cost no great pains; but to set thyself before the Lord, and tie up thy loose and vain thoughts to a constant and serious attendance upon him; this will cost thee something: to attain a facility and dexterity of language in prayer, and put thy meaning into apt and decent expressions, is easy; but to get thy heart broken for sin, while thou art confessing it; melted with free grace, while thou art blessing God for it; to be really ashamed and humbled through the apprehensions of God's infinite holiness, and to keep thy heart in this frame, not only in, but after duty, will surely cost thee some groans and travailing pains of

soul: to repress the outward acts of sin and compose the external part of thy life in a laudable and comely manner, is no great matter; even carnal persons by the force of common principles can do this; but to kill the root of corruption within, to set and keep up an holy government over thy thoughts, to have all things lie straight and orderly in the heart, this is not easy.

2. It is a constant work. The keeping of the heart is such a work as is never done till life be done; this labor and our life end together: it is with a Christian in this business as it is with seamen that have sprung a leak at sea; if they tug not constantly at the pump, the water increases upon them, and will quickly sink them. It is in vain for them to say, the work is hard, and we are weary; there is no time or condition in the life of a Christian which will suffer an intermission of this work. It is in the keeping watch over hearts, as it was in the keeping up of Moses' hands, while Israel and Amalek were fighting below. (Ex. 17:12.) No sooner do Moses' hands grow heavy and sink down, but Amalek prevails. You know it cost David and Peter many a sad day and night for intermitting the watch over their own hearts but a few minutes.

3. It is the most important business of a

Christian's life. Without this we are but formalists in religion; all our professions, gifts and duties signify nothing: "My son, give me thine heart" (Prov. 23:36). God is pleased to call that a gift which is indeed a debt; he will put this honor upon the creature to receive it from him in the way of a gift: but, if this be not given him, he regards not whatever else you bring to him; there is so much only of worth and value in what we do, as there is of heart in it. Concerning the heart, God seems to say, as Joseph of Benjamin, "If you bring not Benjamin with you, you shall not see my face." Among the heathens, when the beast was cut up for sacrifice, the first thing the priest looked upon was the heart; and, if that were unsound and naught, the sacrifice was rejected. God rejects all duties (how glorious soever in other respects) offered him without a heart. He that performs duty without a heart, *viz.,* heedlessly, is no more accepted with God than he that performs it with a double heart, *viz.,* hypocritically (Isa. 66:3). And thus I have briefly opened the nature of the duty, what is imparted in this phrase, "Keep thy heart."

Secondly. Next, I shall give you some rational account why Christians should make this the great business of their lives, to keep their hearts.

7

The importance and necessity of making this our great and main business, will manifestly appear in that; 1. the honor of God; 2. the sincerity of our profession; 3. the beauty of our conversation; 4. the comfort of our souls; 5. the improvement of our graces; and 6. our stability in the hour of temptation; are all wrapt up in, and dependent on, our sincerity and care in the management of this work.

1. The glory of God is much concerned therein; heart-evils are very provoking evils to the Lord. The schools do well observe, that outward sins are sins of great infamy; but heart-sins are sins of deeper guilt. How severely hath the great God declared his wrath from heaven against heart-wickedness; the great crime for which the old world stands indicted, is heart-wickedness. "God saw that every imagination (or fiction) of their heart was only evil, and that continually"; for which he sent the most dreadful judgment that was ever executed since the world began: "And the Lord said, I will destroy man whom I have created from the face of the earth, both man and beast, and the creeping things, and the fowls of heaven, for it repenteth me that I have made man" (Gen. 6:5, 6, 7). We find not their murders, adulteries, blasphemies (tho they were defiled

with these), particularly alleged against them, but the evils of their hearts: yea, that which God was so provoked by, as to give up his peculiar inheritance into the enemy's hand, was the evil of their hearts. "O Jerusalem, wash thine heart from wickedness, that thou mayest be saved; how long shall vain thoughts lodge within thee?" (Jer. 4:14). The wickedness of vanity of their thoughts God took special notice of; and because of this the Chaldean must come upon them as a "lion from his thicket, and tear them to pieces" (Jer. 4:7). For the very sin of thoughts it was that God threw down the fallen angels from heaven, and keeps them still in everlasting chains to the judgment of the great day; by which expression is not obscurely intimated some extraordinary judgment to which they are reserved, as prisoners that have most irons laid upon them, may be supposed to be the greatest malefactors: and what was their sin? Why only spiritual wickedness. For they having no bodily organs, could act nothing externally against God. Yea, mere heart-evils are so provoking, that for them he rejects with indignation all the duties that some men perform unto him. "He that killeth an ox is as if he slew a man; he that sacrificeth a lamb, as if he cut off a dog's neck; he that offered an oblation, as if he offered swine's blood; he that burneth incense, as if he blest an idol'' (Isa. 66:3). In what words could the abhorrence of a creature's actions be more fully exprest by the holy God? Murder and idolatry are not more vile in his account than their sacrifices, tho materially such as himself appointed: and what made them so? The following words inform us; ''Their soul delighteth in their abomination.''

To conclude, such is the vileness of mere heart-sins, that the Scriptures sometimes intimate the difficulty of pardon for them. So in the case of Simon Magus (Acts 8:21), his heart was not right, he had vile thoughts of God and the things of God; the apostle bids him ''repent and pray, if perhaps the thoughts of his heart might be forgiven him.'' O then never slight heart-evils! for by these God is highly wronged and provoked; and for this reason let every Chrisian make it his work to keep his heart with all diligence.

2. The sincerity of our profession much depends upon the care and conscience we have in keeping our hearts; for it is most certain that a man is but a hypocrite in his profession, how curious soever he be in the externals of religion, that is heedless and careless of the frame of his heart: you have a pregnant instance of this in the case of Jehu: ''But Jehu took no heed to walk in the

ways of the Lord God of Israel with his heart'' (2 Kings 10:31). That context gives us an account of the great service performed by Jehu against the house of Ahab and Baal, as also of a great temporal reward given him by God for that service, even that his children to the fourth generation should sit upon the throne of Israel. And yet in these words Jehu is censured for an hypocrite: tho God approved, and rewarded the work, yet he abhorred and rejected the person that did it as hypocritical: and wherein lay his hypocrisy? but in this, that he took no heed to walk in the ways of the Lord with his heart, *i.e.*, he did all insincerely, and for self-ends; and tho the work he did was materially good, yet he, not purging his heart from those unworthy self-designs in doing it, was an hypocrite: and Simon, of whom we spake before, tho he appeared such a person that the apostle could not regularly refuse him; yet his hypocrisy was quickly discovered: and what discovered it but this, that tho he profest and associated himself with the saints, yet he was a stranger to the mortification of heart-sins! "Thy heart is not right with God'' (Acts 8:21). It is true, there is a great difference among Christians themselves, in their diligence and dexterity about heart-work; some are more conversant and successful in it than others are; but he that takes no heed to his heart, that he is not careful to order it aright before God, is but a hypocrite. "And they came unto me as the people cometh, and sit before thee (as my people) and hear thy words, but they will not do them; for with their mouths they show much love, but their heart goes after their covetousness" (Ezek. 33:31, 32). Here was a company of formal hypocrites, as is evident by that expression ("as my people") like them, but not of them. And what made them so? Their outside was fair; here were reverend postures, high profession, much seeming joy and delight in ordinances, "thou art to them as a lovely song"; yea, but for all that they kept not their hearts with God in those duties, their hearts were commanded by their lusts, they went after their covetousness; had they kept their hearts with God, all had been well; but not regarding which way their hearts went in duty, where lay the core of their hypocrisy.

Objection: If any upright soul should hence infer that I am an hypocrite too, for many times my heart departs from God in duty, do what I can; yet I can not hold it close with God.

Solution: To this I answer, the very objection carries in it its own solution. Thou sayest, do what I can, yet I can not keep my heart with God. Soul, if thou doest what thou canst, thou hast the blessing of an upright, tho God sees good to exercise thee under the affliction of a discomposed heart. There remains still some wildness in the thoughts and fancies of the best to humble them; but if you find a care before to prevent them, and opposition against them when they come, grief and sorrow afterward; you will find enough to clear you from reigning hypocrisy.

First, this fore-care is seen partly in laying up the word in thine heart to prevent them, "Thy word have I hid in mine heart, that I might not sin against thee" (Ps. 119:11): Partly in our endeavors to engage our hearts to God (Jer. 30:21), and partly in begging preventing grace from God in our onsets upon duty (Ps. 119:36, 37), it is a good sign where this care goes before a duty.

And, Second, it is a sweet sign of uprightness to oppose them in their first rise. "I hate vain thoughts" (Ps. 119:113). "The spirit lusteth against the flesh" (Gal. 5:17).

And, Third, thy after-grief discovers thy upright heart. If, with Hezekiah, thou art humbled for the evils of thy heart, thou hast no reason, from those disorders, to question the integrity of it; but to suffer sin to lodge quietly in the heart, to let thy heart habitually and uncontrolledly wander from God, is a sad, and dangerous symptom indeed.

3. The beauty of our conversation arises from the heavenly frame and holy order of our spirits; there is a spiritual luster and beauty in the conversation of saints; "The righteous is more excellent than his neighbor:" they shine as the lights of the world; but whatever luster and beauty is in their lives, comes from the excellency of their spirits, as the candle within puts a luster upon the lantern in which it shines. It is impossible that a disordered and neglected heart should ever produce a well-ordered conversation; and since (as the text observes) the issues or streams of life flow out of the heart as their fountain, it must needs follow, that such as the heart is, the life will be: hence (I Pet. 2:12), "Abstain from fleshly lusts—having your conversation honest," or beautiful, as the Greek word imports. So (Isa. 55:7), "Let the wicked forsake his way, and the unrighteous man his thoughts." His way notes the course of his life, his thoughts the frame of his heart; and therefore since the way and course of his life flows from his thoughts, or the frame of his heart, both or neither will be

forsaken: the heart is the womb of all actions: these actions are virtually and seminally contained in our thoughts, and these thoughts being once made up into affections, are quickly made out into suitable actions and practises. If the heart be wicked, then, as Christ saith, "Out of the heart proceed evil thoughts, murders, adulteries," etc. (Matt. 15:19). Mark the order; first wanton, or revengeful thoughts; then unclean, or murderous practises.

And if the heart be holy and spiritual, then, as David speaks, from sweet experience, "My heart is (indicting) a good matter, I speak of the things which (I have made) my tongue is as the pen of a ready writer" (Ps. 45:1). Here is a life richly beautified with good works, some ready made; "I will speak of the things which I have made": others upon the wheel making, my heart is indicting, but both proceeding from the heavenly frame of his heart.

Put but the heart in frame, and the life will quickly discover that it is so. I think it is not very difficult to discern, by the duties and conversations of Christians, what frames their spirits are under; take a Christian in a good frame, and how serious, heavenly, and profitable will his conversations and duties be? What a lovely companion is he during the continuance of it? It would do any one's heart good to be with him at such a time. "The mouth of the righteous speaketh wisdom, and his tongue talketh of judgment, the law of his God is in his heart" (Ps. 37:30, 31).

When the heart is right with God, and full of God, how dexterously and ingeniously will it wind in spiritual discourse, improving every occasion and advantage to some heavenly purpose? Few words run then at the waste spout.

And what else can be the reason why the discourses and duties of many Christians are become so frothy and unprofitable, their communion both with God and one another become as a dry stalk, but because their hearts are neglected? Surely this must be the reason of it, and verily it is an evil greatly to be bewailed; for want of this Christian fellowship it is become a sapless thing; so the attracting beauty that was wont to shine from the conversation of the saints upon the faces and consciences of the world (which if it did not allure, and bring them in love with the ways of God, yet at least left a testimony in their consciences of the excellency of those men and their ways), this is in a great measure lost, to the unspeakable detriment of religion.

Time was, when Christians did carry it at such a rate that the world stood at a gaze at them. Their life and language were of a different strain from others, their tongues discovered them to be Galileans, wherever they came; but now, since vain speculations and fruitless controversies have so much obtained, and heart-work, practical godliness, so much neglected among professors, the case is sadly altered, their discourse is become like other men's; if they come among you now, they may (to allude to Acts 2:6), "hear every man speak in his own language." And truly I have little hope to see this evil redressed, and the credit of religion again repaired, till Christians fall to their old work, till they ply heart-work closer. When the salt of heavenly-mindedness is again cast into the spring, the streams will run clearer and sweeter.

4. The comfort of our souls doth much depend upon the keeping of our hearts; for he that is negligent in attending his own heart is (ordinarily) a great stranger to assurance, and the sweet comforts flowing from it.

Indeed, if the Antinomian doctrine were true, which teaches you to reject all marks and signs for the trial of your conditions, telling you it is only the Spirit that immediately assures you, by witnessing your adoption directly without them; then you might be careless of your hearts, yea, strangers to them, and yet no strangers to comfort: but, since both Scripture and experience do confute this dotage, I hope you will never look for comfort in that unscriptural way. I deny not but it is the work and office of the Spirit to assure you, and yet do confidently affirm, that if ever you attain assurance, in the ordinary way wherein God dispenses it, you must take pains with your own hearts: you may expect your comforts upon easier terms, but I am mistaken if ever you enjoy them upon any other: "Give all diligence, prove yourselves": this is the Scripture way. I remember Mr. Roberts, in his treatise of the covenant, tells us, that he knew a Christian who, in the infancy of his Christianity, so vehemently panted after the infallible assurance of God's love that for a long time together he earnestly desired some voice from heaven, yea, sometimes walking in the solitary fields, earnestly desired some miraculous voice from the trees and stones there: this, after many desires and longings, was denied him; but in time a better was afforded in the ordinary way of searching the word, and his own heart. An instance of the like nature the learned Gerson gives us of one that was driven by temptation upon the very borders of desperation; at last being sweetly settled, and assured, one asked him, how he attained it, he answered: Not by any extraordinary revelation, but by the subjecting his understanding to the Scriptures, and comparing his own heart with them. The Spirit, indeed, assures by witnessing our adoption; and he witnesseth two ways:

First, objectively, *i.e.*, by working those graces in our souls which are the conditions of the promise; and so the Spirit, and his graces in us, are all one: the Spirit of God dwelling in us is a mark of our adoption. Now the Spirit can not be discerned in his essence, but in his operations; and to discern these is to discern the Spirit; and how these should be discerned, without serious searching and diligent watching of the heart, I can not imagine.

Second, The other way of the Spirit's witnessing is effectively, *i.e.*, by irradiating the soul with a grace-discovering light, shining upon his own work; and this in order of nature follows the former work: he first infuses the grace, and then opens the eye of the soul to see it. Now since the heart is the subject of that infused grace, even this way of the Spirit's witnessing also includes the necessity of keeping carefully our own hearts: for,

First, a neglected heart is so confused and dark that the little grace which is in it is not ordinarily discernible: the most accurate and laborious Christians, that take most pains and spend most time about their hearts, do yet find it very difficut to discover the pure and genuine workings of the Spirit there: how then shall the Christian which is (comparatively) negligent and remiss about heart-work be ever able to discover it? Sincerity, which is the thing sought for, lies in the heart like a small piece of gold in the bottom of a river, he that will find it must stay till the water is clear and settled, and then he shall see it sparkling at the bottom. And that the heart may be clear and settled, how much pains and watching, care and diligence will it cost!

Second, God doth not usually indulge lazy and negligent souls with the comforts of assurance; he will not so much as seem to patronize sloth and carelessness; he will give it, but it shall be in his own way: his command hath united our care and comfort together; they are mistaken that think the beautiful child of assurance may be born without pangs; ah! how many solitary hours have the people of God spent in heart-examination! how many times have they looked into the word, and then into their hearts;

sometimes they thought they discovered sincerity, and were even ready to draw forth the triumphant conclusion of assurance; then comes a doubt they can not resolve, and dashes all again: many hopes and fears, doubtings and reasonings, they have had in their own breasts, before they arrived at a comfortable settlement.

To conclude, suppose it possible for a careless Christian to attain assurance, yet it is impossible he should long retain it; as for those whose hearts are filled with the joys of assurance, if extraordinary care be not used, it is a thousand to one if ever they long enjoy it: for a little pride, vanity and carelessness will dash to pieces all that for which they have been laboring a long time, in many a weary duty. Since, then, the joy of our life, the comfort of our souls, rises and falls with our diligence in this work, keep your hearts with all diligence.

5. The improvement of our graces depends on the keeping of our hearts; I never knew grace thrive in a negligent and careless soul; the habits and roots of grace are planted in the heart; and the deeper they are radicated there, the more thriving and flourishing grace is. In Eph. 3:17 we read of "being rooted in grace"; grace in the heart is the root of every gracious work in

the mouth, and of every holy work in the hand (Ps. 116:10; 2 Cor. 4:13). It is true, Christ is the root of a Christian; but Christ is the originating root; and grace a root originated, planted, and influenced by Christ; according as this thrives under divine influences, so the acts of grace are more or less fruitful, or vigorous. Now, in a heart not kept with care and diligence, these fructifying influences are stopt and cut off: multitudes of vanities break in upon it, and devour its strength; the heart is, as it were, the pasture, in which multitudes of thoughts are fed every day; a gracious heart diligently kept, feeds many precious thoughts of God in a day. "How precious are thy thoughts to me, O God! how great is the sum of them? If I should count them, they are more in number than the sand; and when I awake, I am still with thee" (Ps. 139:17). And as the gracious heart feeds and nourishes them, so they refresh and feast the heart. "My soul is filled as with marrow and fatness whilst I think upon thee" (Ps. 63:5, 6). But in the disregarded heart, swarms of vain and foolish thoughts are perpetually working, and jostle out those spiritual ideas and thoughts of God by which the soul should be refreshed.

Besides, the careless heart makes nothing out of any duty or ordinance it performs or attends on, and yet these are the conduits of heaven, from whence grace is watered and made fruitful: a man may go with an heedless spirit from ordinance to ordinance, abide all his days under the choicest teaching, and yet never be improved by them; for heart-neglect is a leak in the bottom, no heavenly influences, how rich soever, abide in that soul (Matt. 13:3, 4). The heart that lies open and common, like the highway, free for all passengers; when the seed fell on it, the fowls came and devoured it. Alas! it is not enough to hear, unless we take heed how we hear; a man may pray, and never be the better, unless he watch unto prayer. In a word, all ordinances, means, and duties are blest unto the improvement of grace, according to the care and strictness we use in keeping our hearts in them.

Lastly, The stability of our souls in the hour of temptation, will be much, according to the care and conscience we have of keeping our hearts; the careless heart is an easy prey to Satan in the hour of temptation, his main batteries are raised against that fort-royal, the heart; if he wins that, he wins all; for it commands the whole man: and alas! how easy a conquest is a neglected heart? It is no more difficult to surprize it than for an enemy to enter that city whose gates are open and unguarded: it is the watchful heart that discovers and suppresses the temptation before it comes to its strength. Divines observe this to be the method in which temptations are ripened, and brought to their full strength.

There is, First, the irritation of the object, or that power it hath to work upon and provoke our corrupt nature; which is either done by the real presence of the object, or else by speculation, when the object (tho absent) is held out by the phantasy before the soul.

Second, then follows the motion of the sensitive appetite, which is stirred and provoked by the phantasy, representing it as a sensual good, as having profit or pleasure in it.

Third, then there is a consultation in the mind about it, deliberating about the likeliest means of accomplishing it.

Fourth, next follows the election, or choice of the will.

Fifth, and lastly, the desire, or full engagement of the will to it; all this may be done in a few moments, for the debates of the soul are quick, and soon ended: when it comes thus far, then the heart is won: Satan hath entered victoriously, and displayed his colors upon the walls of that royal fort; but had the heart been well guarded at first, it had never come to this height; the temptation had been stopt in the first or second act. And indeed there it is stopt easily; for it is in the motions of a tempted soul to sin, as in the motions of a stone falling from the brow of a hill, it is easily stopt at first, but when once it is set agoing, it "acquires strength by the going"; and therefore it is the greatest wisdom in the world to observe the first motions of the heart, to check and stop sin there. The motions of sin are weakest at first: a little care and watchfulness may prevent such mischief now, which the careless heart not heeding, is brought within the power of temptation; as the Syrians were brought blindfolded into the midst of Samaria before they knew where they were.

By this time, reader, I hope thou art fully satisfied how absolutely and necessary a work the keeping of the heart is, it being a duty that wraps up so many dear interests of the soul in it.

Next, according to the method propounded, I proceed to point out those special seasons in the life of a Christian which require and call for our utmost diligence in keeping the heart; for tho (as was observed before) the duty binds *ad semper*, and there is no time or condition of life in which we may be excused from this work; yet there are some signal seasons, critical hours, requiring more than a common vigilance over the heart.

How to Keep the Heart Humble In Prosperity

The first season is the time of prosperity, when providence smiles upon us, and dandles us upon its knee. Now Christian, keep thy heart with all diligence; for now it will be exceeding apt to grow secure, proud, and earthly: to see a man humble in prosperity is one of the greatest rarities in the world, saith Bernard. Even a good Hezekiah could not hide a vainglorious temper under his temptation, and hence that caution to Israel: "And it shall be when the Lord thy God shall have brought thee into the land which he sware to thy fathers, to Abraham, Isaac, and Jacob, to give thee great and goodly cities which thou buildest not, and houses full of all good things which thou filledst not, etc. Then beware lest thou forget the Lord" (Deut. 6:10, 11, 12). And indeed so it fell out, for "Jeshurun waxed fat, and kicked" (Deut. 32:15).

Now then, the first case will be this, *viz.*

Case 1. How a Christian may keep his heart from pride and carnal security, under the smiles of providence and confluence of creature-comforts?

There are seven choice helps to secure the heart from the dangerous snares of prosperity; the first is this,

1. To consider the dangerous ensnaring temptations attending a pleasant and prosperous condition; few, yea, very few of those that live in the pleasures and prosperity of this world escape everlasting perdition. "It is easier (saith Christ) for a camel to pass through the eye of a needle, than for a rich man to enter into the kingdom of heaven" (Matt. 19:24); and "not many mighty, not many noble are called" (1 Cor. 1:26). It might justly make us tremble when the Scripture tells us in general, that few shall be saved; much more when it tells us, of that rank and sort of which we are, but few shall be saved. When Joshua called all the tribes of Israel to lot upon them for the discovery of Achan, doubtless Achan feared; when the tribe of Judah was taken, his fear increased; but when the family of the Zarhites was taken, it was time then to tremble. So when the Scriptures comes so near as to tell us that of such a sort of men very few shall escape, it is time to look about; saith Chrysostom—"I should wonder if any of the rulers be saved." O how many have been coached to

hell in the chariots of earthly pleasures, while others have been whipt to heaven by the rod of affliction! how few, like the daughter of Tyre, come to Christ with a gift! how few among the rich entreat his favor!

2. It may yet keep us more humble and watchful in prosperity, if we consider that among Christians many have been much the worse for it. How good had it been for some of them if they had never known prosperity! When they were in a low condition, how humble, spiritual, and heavenly were they! but when advanced, what an apparent alteration hath been upon their spirits? It was so with Israel, when they were in a low condition in the wilderness; then Israel was "holiness to the Lord" (Jer. 2:23), but when they came into Canaan, and were fed in a flat pasture, then "we are Lords, we will come no more unto thee" (Jer. 2:3). Outward gains are ordinarily attended with inward losses; as in a low condition their civil employments were wont to have a tang and savor of their duties; so in an exalted condition their duties commonly have a tang of the world. He, indeed, is rich in grace whose graces are not hindered by his riches; there are but few Jehosaphats in the world, of whom it is said, "He had silver and gold in abundance, and his heart was lifted up in the way

of God's commands" (2 Chron. 17:5, 6). Will not this keep thy heart humble in prosperity, to think how dear many godly men have paid for their riches, that through them they have lost that which all the world can not purchase? Then, in the next place,

3. Keep down thy vain heart by this consideration, that God values no man a jot the more for these things. God values no man by outward excellencies, but by inward graces; they are the internal ornaments of the spirit, which are of great price in God's eyes (1 Pet. 3:4). He despises all worldly glory, and accepts no man's person; "but in every nation, he that feareth God, and worketh righteousness, is accepted of him" (Acts 10:35). Indeed, if the judgment of God went by the same rule that man's doth, we might value ourselves by these things, and stand upon them: but, as one said (when dying), I shall not appear before God as a doctor, but as a man. So much every man is and no more, as he is in the judgment of God. Doth thy heart yet swell? And will neither of the former considerations keep it humble?

4. Then, fourthly, consider how bitterly many persons have bewailed their folly when they came to die, that ever they set their hearts upon these things, and heartily wish that they had never known them—What a

sad story was that of Pius Quintus, who dying, cried out despairingly: When I was in a low condition, I had some hopes of salvation; but when I was advanced to be a cardinal, I greatly doubted it; but since I came to the popedom, I have no hope at all. Mr. Spencer also tells us a real but sad story of a rich oppressor, who had scraped up a great estate for his only son; when he came to die, he called his son to him and said, Son, do you indeed love me? The son answered, that nature, besides his paternal indulgence, obliged him to that. Then, said the father, express it by this; hold thy finger in the candle as long as I am saying a *Pater Noster*. The son attempted, but could not endure it. Upon that, the father broke out into these expressions, thou canst not suffer the burning of thy finger for me, but to get this wealth, I have hazarded my soul for thee, and must burn body and soul in hell for thy sake: thy pains would have been but for a moment, but mine will be unquenchable fire.

5. The heart may be kept humble, by considering of what a clogging nature earthly things are to a soul heartily engaged in the way to heaven; they shut out much of heaven from us at present, tho they may not shut us out of heaven at last. If thou consider thyself under the notion of a stranger

in this world, traveling for heaven and seeking a better country, thou hast then as much reason to be taken and delighted with these things as a weary horse hath with a heavy load: there was a serious truth in that atheistical scoff of Julian, when he took away the Christians' estate, and told them it was to make them fitter for the kingdom of heaven.

6. Is thy spirit, for all this, flatulent and lofty? Then urge upon it the consideration of that awful day of reckoning, wherein, according to our receipts of mercies, shall be our accounts for them: and methinks this should awe, and humble the vainest heart that ever was in the breast of a saint. Know for certain, that the Lord records all the mercies that ever he gave thee, from the beginning to the end of thy life. "Remember, O my people, from Shittim unto Gilgal," etc. (Micah 6:4). Yea, they are exactly numbered, and recorded in order to an account; and thy account will be suitable. "To whomsoever much is given, of him much shall be required" (Luke 12:48). You are but stewards, and your Lord will come to take an account of you; and what a great account have you to make, who have much of this world in your hands? What swift witnesses will your mercies be against you, if this be the best fruits of them?

7. It is a very humbling consideration, that the mercies of God should work otherwise upon my spirit than they use to do upon the spirits of others, to whom they come as sanctified mercies from the love of God. Ah Lord! what a sad condition is this! Enough to lay me in the dust, when I consider,

First, that their mercies have greatly humbled them; the higher God has raised them, the lower they have laid themselves before God. Thus did Jacob, when God had given him much substance. "And Jacob said, I am not worthy of the least of all thy mercies, and all the truth which thou hast shewed thy servants; for with my staff I passed over this Jordan, and am now become two bands" (Gen. 32:10). And thus it was with holy David (2 Sam. 7:18). When God had confirmed the promise to him, to build him a house, and not reject him as he did Saul, he goes in before the Lord, and saith, "Who am I? and what is my father's house, that thou hast brought me hitherto?" And so indeed God required (Deut. 26:5), when Israel was to bring to God the first-fruits of Canaan, they were to say, "a Syrian ready to perish was my father," etc. Do others raise God the higher for the raising them? And the more God raises me, the more shall

I abuse him, and exalt myself? O what a sad thing is this?

Second, others have freely ascribed the glory of all their enjoyments to God, and magnified not themselves, but him, for their mercies: so David (2 Sam. 7:26): "Let thy name be magnified, and the house of thy servant be established." He doth not fly upon the mercy, and suck out the sweetness of it, looking no farther than his own comfort; no, he cares for no mercy except God be magnified in it. So (Ps. 18:2) when God had delivered him from all his enemies: "The Lord (saith he) is my strength, and my rock, he is become my salvation." They did not put the crown upon their own heads, as I do.

Third, the mercies of God have been melting mercies unto others, melting their souls in love to the God of their mercies. So Hannah (1 Sam 2:1), when she had received the mercy of a son, "My soul (saith she) rejoiceth in the Lord"; not in the mercy, but in the God of the mercy. And so Mary, "My soul doth magnify the Lord, my spirit rejoiceth in God my Savior" (Luke 1:46). The word signifies to make more room for God; their hearts were not contracted, but the more enlarged to God.

Fourth, the mercies of God have been mighty restraints to keep others from sin. So

Ezra (9:13), "Seeing thou, our God, hast given us such a deliverance as this, should we again break thy commandments?" Ingenuous souls have felt the force of the obligations of love and mercy upon them.

Fifth, to conclude, the mercies of God to others have been as oil to the wheels of their obedience, and made them fitter for services (2 Chron. 17:5). Now if mercies work contrarily upon my heart, what cause have I to be afraid that they come not to me in love? I tell you, this is enough to damp the spirit of any saint, to see what sweet effects they have had on others, and what sad effects on him.

How to Keep the Heart In Time of Adversity

The second special season in the life of a Christian requiring more than a common diligence to keep his heart in the time of adversity. When providence frowns upon you, and blasts your outward comforts, then look to your hearts, keep them with all diligence from repining against God, or fainting under his hand; for troubles, tho sanctified, are troubles still; even sweetbriar and holy thistle have their prickles. Jonah was a good man, and yet how pettish was his heart under affliction? Job was the mirror of patience, yet how was his heart discomposed by troubles? You will find it as hard to get a composed spirit under great afflictions as it is to fix quicksilver. O the hurries and tumults which they occasion even in the best hearts! Well then, the second case will be this:

Case 2. How a Christian under great afflictions may keep his heart from repining or desponding under the hand of God? Now there are nine special helps I shall here offer to keep thy heart in this condition; and the first shall be this, to work upon your hearts this great truth:

Help 1. That by these cross providences, God is faithfully pursuing the great design of electing love upon the souls of his people, and orders all these afflictions as means sanctified to that end.

Afflictions fall not out by casualty, but by counsel (Job. 5:6; Eph. 1:11); by this counsel of God they are ordained as means of much spiritual good to saints (Isa. 27:9). "By this shall the iniquity of Jacob be purged" (Heb. 12:10). "But he for our profit," etc. (Rom. 8:28). "All things work together for our good." They are God's workmen upon our hearts, to pull down the pride and carnal security of them; and being so, their nature is changed; they are turned into blessings and benefits. It is good for me that I have been afflicted (Ps. 119:71). And sure, then, thou hast no reason to quarrel with, but rather so admire that God should concern himself so much in thy good, to use any means for the accomplishing of it (Phil. 3:11). Paul could bless God, if by any means he might attain the resurrection of the dead. "My brethren (saith James) count it all joy when you fall into divers temptations" (James 1:23). My Father is about a design of love upon my soul, and do I well to be angry with him? All that he doth is in pursuance of, and in reference to some eternal glorious ends upon my soul. O, it is my ignorance of God's design, that makes me quarrel with him! He saith to thee in this case, as to Peter: "What I do thou knowest not now, but hereafter thou shalt know it."

Help 2. Tho God hath reserved to himself a liberty of afflicting his people, yet he hath tied up his own hands by promise never to take away his loving-kindness from them. Can I look that Scripture in the face with a repining, discontented spirit. "I will be his father, and he shall be my son; if he commit iniquity, I will chasten him with the rod of men, and with the stripes of the children of men: nevertheless my mercy shall not depart away from him" (2 Sam. 7:14). O my heart! my haughty heart! dost thou well to be discontented when God hath given thee the whole tree, with all the clusters of comfort growing on it, because he suffers the wind to blow down a few leaves? Christians have two sorts of good, the goods of the throne, and the goods of the foot-stool; movables, and immovables: if God have secured these, never let my heart be troubled at the loss of those; indeed, if he had cut off his love, or discovenanted my soul, I had reason to be cast down; but this he hath not, nor can he do it.

Help 3. It is of marvelous efficacy to keep the heart from sinking under affliction, to call to mind, that thine own Father hath the ordering of them: not a creature moves hand or tongue against thee but by his permission. Suppose the cup be a bitter cup, yet it is the cup which thy Father hath given thee to drink; and canst thou suspect poison to be in that cup which he delivers thee? Foolish man, put home the case to thine own heart, consult with thine own bowels; canst thou find in thy heart to give thy child that which would hurt and undo him? no, thou wouldst as soon hurt thyself as him; "If thou then being evil knowest how to give good gifts to thy children," how much more doth God? (Matt. 7:11). The very consideration of his nature, a God of love, pity and tender mercies, or of his relation to thee, as a father, husband, friend, might be security enough, if he had not spoken a word, to quiet thee in this case; and yet you have his word too (Jer. 25: 6), I will do you no hurt. You lie too near his heart to hurt you; nothing grieves him more than your groundless and unworthy suspicions of his designs do. Would it not grieve a faithful tender-hearted physician, when he hath studied the case of his patient, prepared the most excellent receipts to save his life, to hear him cry out, O he hath undone me! he hath poisoned me; because it gripes and pains him in the operation? O when will you be ingenuous.

Help 4. God respects you as much in a low, as in a high condition; and therefore it need not so much trouble you to be made low; nay, to speak home, he manifests more of his love, grace, and tenderness, in the time of affliction, than prosperity. As God did not at first choose you because you were high, so he will not forsake you because you are low; men may look shy upon you, and alter their respects, as your condition is altered: when providence hath blasted your estates, your summer friends may grow strange, as fearing you may be troublesome to them; but will God do so? No, no, "I will never leave thee, nor forsake thee" (Heb. 13:

5). Indeed if adversity and poverty could bar you from access to God, it were a sad condition; but you may go to God as freely as ever. "My God (saith the Church) will hear me" (Micah 7). Poor David, when stript of all earthly comforts, could yet encourage himself in the Lord his God, and why can not you? Suppose your husband or child had lost all at sea, and should come to you in rags, could you deny the relation, or refuse to entertain him? If you would not, much less will God: why then are you so troubled? tho your condition be changed, your Father's love and respects are not changed.

Help 5. And what if, by the loss of outward comforts, God will preserve your souls from the ruining power of temptation? Sure then, you have little cause to sink your hearts by such sad thoughts about them. Are not these earthly enjoyments the things that make men shrink and warp in times of trial? For the love of these many have forsaken Christ in such an hour. "He went away sorrowful, for he had great possessions" (Matt. 19:22). And if this be God's design, what have I done in quarreling with him about it? We see mariners in a storm can throw overboard rich bales of silk, and precious things, to preserve the vessel and their lives with it, and every one saith they act prudently; we know it is usual for soldiers in a city besieged to batter down or burn the fairest buildings without the walls, in which the enemy may shelter in the siege, and no man doubts but it is wisely done: such as have gangrened legs or arms can willingly stretch them out to be cut off, and not only thank but pay the surgeon for his pains: and must God only be repined at, for casting over what will sink you in a storm? For pulling down that which would advantage your enemy in the siege of temptation? For cutting off what would endanger your everlasting life? O inconsiderate, ungrateful man! are not these things, for which thou grievest, the very things that have ruined thousands of souls? Well, what Christ doth in this thou knowest not now, but hereafter thou mayest.

Help 6. It would much stay the heart under adversity, to consider, that God by such humbling providences may be accomplishing that for which you have long prayed and waited: and should you be troubled at that? Say, Christian, hast thou not many prayers depending before God upon such accounts as these; that he would keep thee from sin, discover to thee the emptiness and insufficiency of the creature; that he would kill and mortify thy lusts, that thy heart may never find rest in any enjoyment but Christ? Why now, by such humbling and impoverishing strokes, God may be fulfilling thy desire: wouldst thou be kept from sin? "Lo, he hath hedged up thy way with thorns." Wouldst thou see the creature's vanity? Thy affliction is a fair glass to discover it, for the vanity of the creature is never so effectually and sensibly discovered, as in our own experience of it. Wouldst thou have thy corruptions mortified? This is the way; now God takes away the food and fuel that maintained them; for as prosperity begot and fed them, so adversity, when sanctified, is a means to kill them. Wouldst thou have thy heart to rest nowhere but in the bosom of God? What better way canst thou imagine providence should take to accomplish thy desire than by pulling from under thy head that soft pillow of creature delights on which thou rested before? And yet you fret at this, peevish child. How dost thou exercise thy Father's patience! If he delay to answer thy prayers, thou art ready to say he regards thee not; if he do that which really answers the scope and main end of them, but not in the way thou expected, thou quarrelleth with him for that: as if, instead of answering, he were crossing all thy hopes and aims. Is this ingenuous? Is it not enough that God is so gracious to do what thou desirest, but thou must be so imprudent to expect he should do it in the way which thou prescribest.

Help 7. Again, it may stay thy heart, if thou consider, that in these troubles God is about that work which, if thou didst see the design of, thy soul would rejoice. We, poor creatures, are bemisted with such ignorance, and are not able to discern how particular providences work toward God's end; and therefore, like Israel in the wilderness, are often murmuring, because providence leads us about in a howling desert, where we are exposed to straits; tho yet, then he led them, and is now leading us, "by the right way, to a city of habitations." If you could but see how God, in his secret council, hath exactly laid the whole plot and design of thy salvation, even to the smallest means and circumstances; this way, and by these means, such a one shall be saved, and by no other; such a number of afflictions I appoint for this man, at this time, and in this order; they shall befall him thus, and thus they shall work for him. Could you, I say, but discern the admirable harmony of divine dispensations, their mutual relations to each other, together with the general respect and influence they all have into the last end; of all the conditions in the world you would choose that you are now in, had you liberty to make your choice.

Providence is like a curious piece of arras, made up of a thousand shreds, which single we know not what to make of, but put together, and stitched up orderly, they represent a beautiful history to the eye. As God works all things according to the counsel of his own will, so that counsel of God hath ordained this as the best way to bring about thy salvation: such a one hath a proud heart, so many humbling providences I appoint for him; such a one an earthly heart, so many impoverishing providences for him: did you but see this, I need say no more to support the most dejected heart.

Help 8. Further, it would much conduce to the settlement of your hearts to consider, That by fretting and discontent, you do yourself more injury than all the afflictions you lie under could do; your own discontent is that which arms your troubles with a sting, it is you that make your burden heavy, by struggling under it. Could you but lie quiet under the hand of God, your condition would be much easier and sweeter than it is. This makes God lay on more strokes, as a father will upon a stubborn child that receiveth not correction.

Besides, it unfits the soul to pray over its troubles, or take in the sense of that good which God intends by them: affliction is a pill, which, being wrapt up in patience and quiet submission, may be easily swallowed; but discontent chews up the pill, and so embitters the soul: God throws away some comfort which he saw would hurt you, and you will throw away your peace after it; he shoots an arrow which sticks in your clothes and was never intended to hurt, but only to fright you from sin, and you will thrust it onward to the piercing of your very hearts, by despondency and discontent.

Help 9. Lastly, if all this will not do, but thy heart, like Rachel, still refuses to be comforted or quieted, then consider one thing more, which, if seriously pondered, will doubtless do the work; and that is this, Compare the condition thou art now in (and art so much dissatisfied with) with that condition others are, and thyself deservest to be in: others are roaring in flames, howling under the scourge of vengeance, and amongst them I deserve to be. O my soul! is this hell? Is my condition as bad as the damned? O what would thousands now in hell give to change conditions with me!

It is a famous instance which Dr. Taylor gives us of the duke of Condé; I have read (saith he) that when the duke of Condé had entered voluntarily into the incommodities of a religious poverty, he was one day espied and pitied by a lord of Italy, who out of tenderness wished him to be more careful and nutritive of his person. The good duke answered, Sir, be not troubled, and think not that I am ill provided for conveniences, for I send an harbinger before me, who makes ready my lodgings, and takes care that I be royally entertained. The lord asked him who was his harbinger? He answered, The knowledge of myself, and the consideration of what I deserve for my sins, which is eternal torments; and when with this knowledge I arrive at my lodging, how unprovided soever I find it, methinks it is even better than I deserve. Why doth the living man complain? And thus the heart may be kept from desponding or repining under adversity.

[The remaining chapters are: 3. How the heart may be supported in time of Zion's troubles; 4. How it may be preserved from fears in public dangers; 5. How it may be kept from repining when outward wants are either felt or feared; 6. How it may be kept from vain thoughts in religious duties; 7. How it may be kept from revengeful motions under injuries; 8. How it may be kept meek and patient under great provocations; 9. How it may be kept when tempted, from yielding to the temptations; 10. How it may be kept from sad conclusions in dark and doubting seasons; 11. How it may be kept from relapsing under sufferings for religion; 12. How it may be reconciled to death in time of sickness.]

A Prayer of S. Weiss

O God, our Lord, the Stay of all them that put their trust in thee, wherever thou leadest we would go, for thy ways are perfect wisdom and love. Even when we walk through the dark valley, thy light can shine into our hearts and guide us safely through the night of sorrow. Be thou our Friend, and we need ask no more in heaven or earth; for thou art the comfort of all who trust in thee, the help and defense of all who hope in thee. O Lord, we would be thine; let us never fall away from thee. We would accept all things without murmuring from thy hand, for whatever thou dost is right. Blend our wills with thine, and then we need fear no evil nor death itself, for all things must work together for our good. Lord keep us in thy love and truth; comfort us with thy light, and guide us by thy Holy Spirit. AMEN.

SELECTIONS FROM

Reason and Religion
or
The Grounds and Measures of Devotion

Considered From the Nature of God, and the Nature of Man

In Several Contemplations

With Exercises of Devotion Applied to Every Contemplation

BY

JOHN NORRIS, M.A.

JOHN NORRIS

English clergyman and one of the most prolific writers of his time, was born at Collingbourne-Kingston, Wiltshire, 1657; died at Bemerton, Wiltshire, 1711. He was educated at Winchester School and Exeter College, Oxford (B. A., 1680), and was later appointed a fellow of All Souls' (M. A., 1684). From 1692 until his death he was rector of Bemerton, the parish earlier held by George Herbert. His works represent the teaching of Plato and Malebranche. In his "Essay towards the Theory of an Ideal and Intelligible World" (1701-4) he combatted Locke's theories. Among his other works may be mentioned "Reason and Religion, or the Grounds and Measures of Devotion . . . in several Contemplations, with Exercises of Devotion applied to every Contemplation," 1689; "A Philosophical Discourse Concerning the Natural Immortality of the Soul," 1708. His most popular work is "A Collection of Miscellanies, consisting of Poems, Essays, Discourses, and Letters," Oxford, 1687.

Reason and Religion; or, The Grounds and Measures of Devotion

[The author's method is to discuss certain themes, to show the value of the conclusions to devotion, and then to sum up the discussion and express it devotionally in "The Aspirations," which last are given below, together with the themes to which they are related. The author's view of devotion, contemplation, and knowledge is given in the three selections from the Introduction.]

[The original spelling has been retained in this selection.]

PART I

Introduction

VIII

By devotion here I do not meerly understand that special disposition or act of the soul, whereby we warmly and passionately address ourselves to God in prayer (which is what is commonly meant by devotion); but I use the word in a greater latitude, so as to comprehend under it faith, hope, love, fear, trust, humility, submission, honour, reverence, adoration, thanksgiving, in a word, all that duty which we owe to God. Nor by this acceptation do I stretch the word beyond what either from its rise it may or, by frequent use among the learned, it does signifie. Devotion is *a devovendo,* from devoting, or giving up ones self wholly to the service of another. And accordingly those among the heathens who deliver'd and consign'd themselves up to death, for the safety of their country, were called *devoti.* And so in like manner for a man to give up himself wholly and intirely to the service of God, and actually to demean himself towards him in the conduct of his life, as becomes a creature towards his Creator, is devotion.

XI

To shew how much contemplation serves to the advantage of devotion, we need only consider that devotion is an act of the will, that the object of the will is good apparent, or good understood, and consequently that every act of the will is influenc'd and regulated by consideration. Devotion therefore is as much influenc'd by consideration as any other act of the will is.

XII

I deny not but that knowledge and devotion often go assunder, and the wisest are not always the devoutest. But then this is not owing to the natural and direct influence of knowledge, but comes to pass only occasionally and accidentally, by reason of some other impediment: suppose pride, lust, covetousness, or some such disposition of mind, which is of more force and prevalency to lett our devotion, than knowledge is to further it. And then no wonder that the heavier scale weighs down. But still knowledge has a natural aptness to excite devotion, and will infallibly do it if not hinder'd by some other cause. So that we may take this for a never-failing rule, That all other things being equal, the more knowing and considering, still the more devout. And in this sense also that of the psalmist will be verifi'd, while I was musing the fire kindled.

Contemplation I—Of the General Idea of God

The Aspiration

O thou whose name is Jehovah, who art the very essence of being, who art being itself, how can I ever sufficiently love, fear, reverence and adore thee! Thou art above all the affections of my heart, all the motions of my will, yea and all the conceptions of my understanding. No sooner do I begin to think of thee, but I am plunged beyond my depth, my thoughts are all swallow'd up and overwhelm'd in their first approach to thy essence, and I shall sooner lose myself than find thee.

O dreadful Excellence, I tremble to think of thy essence, my soul turns herself from thee, she cannot look forward, she pants, she burns, she languishes, is beaten back with the light of thy glories, and returns to the familiarity of her own darkness, not because she chuses it, but because she is weary.

O soveraign Greatness, how am I impoverish'd, how am I contracted, how am I annihilated in thy presence. Thou only art, I am not, thou art all, I am nothing. But 'tis well, O my God, that I am nothing, so thou art all; 'tis well I am not in myself, so I am in thee.

O Being itself, 'tis in thee that I live, move, and have my being. Out of thee I am nothing. I have nothing, I can do nothing. I am but little and inconsiderable with thee, and what then should I be without thee? To thee therefore I devote and dedicate my whole self, for I am wholly thine. I will ever live to thee, since I must ever live in thee. And Oh let my beloved be ever mine, as I am, and ever will be his. AMEN.

Contemplation II—That God Is a Being Absolutely Perfect Proved from the Preceding General Idea of God

The Aspiration

My Lord and my God, with what awful apprehensions do I contemplate thy perfections! How am I struck, dazled, and confounded with the light of thy glories! Thy being standeth like the strong mountains, and thy perfections are like the great deep. How can I think of thee without wonder and astonishment, and how can I think of anything else but thee!

O thou circle of excellency, thou endless orb of perfection, where shall I begin to love thee? Thou art altogether lovely; oh that I were also altogether love. My God, I desire nothing but to love thee, and to be loved by thee. Thou art all fair, my love, there is no spot in thee. My beloved is light, and in him is no darkness at all; Let him therefore kiss me with the kisses of his mouth, for his love is better than wine.

My great God, how do I despise myself and the whole creation when I once think upon thee! Whom have I in heaven but thee, and there is none upon earth that I desire in comparison of thee. Thou alone dost so fill my thoughts, so ravish my affections, that I can contemplate nothing but thee, I can admire nothing but thee, and I can love nothing but thee. Nor do I think my soul straiten'd in being confined to thee, for thou, O my God art all.

O my God, I have lookt for thee in holiness, that I might behold this thy power and thy glory. I can now see it but in a glass darkly, but thou hast told us that those who are pure in heart shall hereafter see thee face to face. Grant therefore I may so love, fear, and serve thee here, that I may behold thee, and enjoy thee, as thou art in thy infinite self, for ever hereafter. AMEN.

Contemplation III—That Therefore All the Perfections of Particular Beings Exist In God, and that After a More Excellent Manner than They Do In Particular Beings Themselves

The Aspiration

No, my fair Delight, I will never be drawn off from the love of thee by the charms of any of thy creatures. Thou art not only infinitely more excellent than they, but hast their very excellencies in a more perfect manner than they have or can have. What temptation then can I have to leave thee? No, O my fairest, I want temptation to recommend my love to thee. 'Tis too easie and too cheap a fidelity to adhere to thee, my first love, when by changing I can gain no more.

Thou, O Soveraign fair, hast adorn'd thy creation with a tincture of thy brightness, thou hast shin'd upon it with the light of thy divine glory, and hast pour'd forth thy beauty upon all thy works. But they are not fair as thou art fair, their beauty is not as thy beauty. Thou art fairer, O my God, than the children of men, or the orders of angels, and the arrows of thy love are sharper than theirs. They are indeed, my God, thy arrows are very sharp, and were we not too securely fenc'd about with our thick houses of clay, would wound us deeper than the keenest charms of any created beauties. But these every day wound us, while we stand proof against thy divine artillery, because these are sensible, and thine only intelligible; these are visible to our eyes, thine only to our minds, which we seldome convert to the contemplation of thy beauties.

But, O thou infinite fair, did we but once taste and see, did we but contemplate thy original beauty, as we do those faint images of it that are reflected up and down among our fellow creatures, as thy charms infinitely exceed theirs, so would our love to thee be wonderful, passing the love of women.

Contemplation IV—Of the Attributes of God In General; Particularly of the Unity of God: Which Is Proved From His Idea

The Aspiration

O thou mighty One-all, who art too great to be multiplied, and yet too full not to be communicated, what a greatness, what a fulness is this of thine! O rich solitude, how unlike is all created excellence to thine! Other things are to be admired for their numbers, thou for thy oneness and singularity, they glory in their multitudes, but 'tis the prerogative of thy perfection to be alone.

In thee, my only centre, I rest, upon thee I wholly depend, for I have none in heaven but thee, and none upon earth in comparison of thee. I utterly renounce therefore all absolute power and supremacy besides thine, and I will fear none but thee, and obey none but thee. Thou only shalt have dominion over me, I am only thine, and thee only will I serve.

Many, O God, are the beauties which thou hast made, and thy whole creation is fill'd with thy glory. There are threescore queens, and fourscore concubines, and virgins without number; but my love, my undefiled, is but one. Take then to thyself the empire of my heart. For all that deserves the name of love there shall be thine. O that it were more inlarged for thy reception: but thou shalt have it all, and I will love thee with my whole heart, though that whole be but little.

O my only delight, other gods besides thee, and other lords besides thee, have often usurp'd a dominion over me. But my heart is now fix'd, O God, my heart is fix'd. It is fix'd upon thee, and how can it ever wander out of the sphere of thy beauty! Or what beauty is there whose influence may vye with thine? Or how can I love any but one, when that one, and none but that one, is infinitely lovely.

Contemplation V—Of the Omniscience and Omnipresence of God

The Aspiration

[After quoting an early translation of Ps. 139:1-12, the author proceeds.]

Do thou then, O my God, so imprint the sense of this thy omniscience and omnipresence upon every faculty and power of my soul, that I may ever think, speak, and act as in the light of thy all-seeing eye, and as immediately surrounded, and intimately possessed with the glory of thy presence. O fill me with the profoundest awe and reverence, compose my levities, confirm my doubtfulness, and fix my wandrings, and make me ever satisfied with the methods of thy wise providence.

And when by the meditation of this thy knowledge and presence, I shall learn to demean myself in any measure as I ought: grant that upon the same consideration I may content myself with thy divine approbation and allowance, whatever I am thought of in man's judgment. Finally, O my God, grant I may so set thee before me here, that I may not be afraid to appear before thee hereafter. AMEN.

Contemplation VI—Of the Omnipotence of God

The Aspiration

With thee, O my God, is power and strength, and with thee ought to be dominion and fear. My flesh trembles for fear of thee: and I am afraid of thy judgments. Thou art terrible, O my God, as well as lovely, but thou art also lovely in thy very terrour. Turn away thine eyes from me, for they have overcome me; they have overcome me with their dread, as well as with their beauty; for, as thou art beautiful, O my love, as Tirzah, comely, as Jerusalem; so art thou also terrible, as an army with banners.

O my Omnipotent Love, with what safety, as well as delight, do I sit under thy shadow! Thou hast brought me into thy banquetting-house, and thy banner over me is power as well as love. Thy love is stronger than death; what need I fear, thy left hand is under my head, and thy right hand does imbrace me; and why then should any dread approach me? The Lord is my light and my salvation, whom then shall I fear? He is the strength of my life, of whom then should I be afraid.

O, my God, why is not my faith like thy power? Thou canst do all things; and why is my faith limited? Let me imitate thee, O my God, in this thy infinity: and grant me such a victorious, such an omnipotent faith, that, as to thee nothing is too hard to do, so to me nothing may be too hard to believe. AMEN.

Contemplation VII—Of the Divine Justice and Veracity

The Aspiration

My God, my Judge, who art righteous in all thy ways, and holy in all thy works, I delight to think of thee, tho' I am too guilty to contemplate thee, in this thy attribute, without fear and trembling. For there is judgment as well as mercy with thee that thou shouldst be fear'd. O enter not into judgment with thy servant, for in thy sight shall no man living be justify'd.

My God, how strangely impious are they who dare say or think that the way of the Lord is not equal! My God, I am none of those, nor will I ever be of that profane number. I will ever acquiesce in the equity of thy dispensations, whether I am able to comprehend it or no. For I know tho' clouds and darkness may sometimes be round about thee, yet righteousness and judgment are always the habitation of thy seat.

I readily and firmly assent, O my God, to all the declarations thou hast made of thy mind and will. I believe all thy predictions, all thy promises, and all thy threatenings, that they shall be fulfill'd all in their season. I know that nothing but truth can proceed from thee who art truth itself: I know that thou, O God, can'st not deceive us, O grant that we may not deceive ourselves. AMEN.

Contemplation VIII—Of the Divine Goodness and Philanthropy

The Aspiration

O my great and good God, who art good in all thy greatness, and whose chiefest greatness is to be good, how can I possibly think amiss of thee, distrust thee, or harbour any jealous apprehensions concerning thee? And how unworthy should I be of this thy goodness if I should!

But, O God, my love, 'tis my infirmity to be afraid of that excellence which I should rather love, for my love of thee is not yet perfect enough to cast out all fear; but blessed be thy goodness, who in the midst of my fears and doubtful surmises art pleased to remind me of thy nature, and to say to my soul, as thou didst once to the diffident disciples, It is I, be not afraid.

The voice of my beloved! I will therefore turn my fears to love, and love more than I ever yet feared or loved. I will also magnifie thee, O God, my King: and I will praise thy name for ever and ever. Every day will I give thanks unto thee: and praise thy name for ever and ever. For I have tasted and seen how gracious thou art, and I find it is a good thing to praise thee: and that 'tis a joyful and pleasant thing to be thankful. I know, O my God, that thy goodness is as much above my praise as thy greatness is above my comprehension. My praises can add nothing to thee, neither can I praise thee according to thy goodness. But, O my God, I will praise thee according to my strength, and I know that the same goodness of thine, which is too great to be praised worthily, is also too great not to accept our unworthy praises.

My God, I know thou requirest from me only the praises of a man, but I am troubled that I cannot praise thee as an angel. O that I were now in heaven, if 'twere only that I might praise thee as thy angels praise thee: this, O my God, I will do hereafter, my gratitude shall run then as high as theirs, and it shall be lasting too; it shall last as long as thy goodness and my being lasts; and as thy mercy, so my praise shall endure for ever.

John Norris

PART II

Wherein the Grounds and Measures of Devotion Are Consider'd From the Nature of Man

Contemplation I—Of Man, Consider'd as a Creature

The Aspiration

My God, my Creator, how can I be ever sufficiently humble, when I consider that I once was not; when I consider that even thou with all thy omnipotence can'st not reduce me to a lower degree of nothing than that from whence thou took'st me! When I consider that I still so depend upon thee, that I cannot subsist one moment without thee! What a vanity, what a shadow, what a nothing then am I, who once was not, and now am only because thou art, and can no longer stand in being than supported by the arm of thy power!

O my God, I know not whether of the two I ought more to adore and magnifie, either that power that could raise me from nothing, to be what I am, or that goodness which could determine that power to so strange and wonderful a production. One deep, O my God, calleth upon another, and my thoughts are all lost and swallow'd up in both.

Praise and adoration be to thee, O my great and good God for 'twas from thy power and goodness that I receiv'd my being. Thou art he that took me out of my mother's womb, and thou also wast my hope when I hanged yet upon my mother's breast. I have been also left unto thee ever since I was born: thou art my God even from my mother's womb. My soul still hangeth upon thee: thy right hand does uphold me. Thou holdest my soul in life, and sufferest not my feet to slip.

To thee then, O Father of spirits, I give up and devote my whole self, for I am intirely from thee, intirely by thee, and therefore intirely thine. How then can I ever offend thee, or rebel against thee, with those powers which thou hast given me, and dost still uphold and maintain in me! My God, I will not, but as thou art he whose I am, so thou shalt be he whom I will ever serve. Free me therefore, O God, from my passions, and make me but once my own, and I will then ever be thine. AMEN.

Contemplation II—Of Man Consider'd as an Intelligent Creature

The Aspiration

My God, my Light, what is man that thou art mindful of him, and the son of man that thou so regardest him? But much more, what is man that he should so regard himself? that he should regard himself for that which is least of all his own, his knowledge and wisdom? For, O God, we are not a light to ourselves, but 'tis thou, O God, art our light, and in thy light do we see light.

O my wonderful counsellour, with what humility and poverty of spirit ought I to reflect upon the richest endowments of my mind, since I see only by thy light, and depend upon thee for what I know, as much as for what I am: and how unworthy should I be of thy divine light, should I be puffed up through the abundance of this thy revelation.

Not unto me therefore, O my God, my Light, not unto me, but to thy greatness and goodness be the praise and the glory. For 'tis thy word, thy eternal word, that is a lantern unto my feet, and a light unto my paths. The Lord is my light and my salvation, and it is he that teacheth man knowledge. I will therefore thank the Lord for giving me warning, my reins also chasten me in the night-season.

Lighten my darkness then, I beseech, O Father of lights, and shine upon me more and more with the brightness of thy glory. O send out thy light and thy truth, that they may lead me, and bring me unto thy holy hill, and to thy dwelling.

Shew the light of thy countenance upon thy servant, and teach me thy statutes. O let the angel of thy presence go always before me in this my pilgrimage, and grant that I may always attend and give heed to his counsel and direction, that so walking in thy light here, I may forever live, and forever rejoyce in the full and open light of thy countenance hereafter. AMEN.

Contemplation III—Of Man, Consider'd as an Amorous Creature

The Aspiration

My God, my Love, how absurd a thing it is that an amorous creature should be a proud creature! My love is occasion'd by my indigence, and I cannot love but I am minded of that indigence; how ill then would pride become me, having so much reason to be humble, and that reason so continually set before me!

Divine Fountain of love, 'tis from thee I receive all my love, and upon whom should I place it but upon thee? The fire that descends from heaven, where should it be spent but upon the altar? Thou hast a right, O my God to all my love, for I cannot love thee with any love but what is thy own. O then do thou regulate this thy own divine impression, and grant I may never sin against thee by the abuse of that love which thou hast given me. I thank thee, O Father, Lord of heaven and earth, for doing so much towards the guidance and regulation of my love as to carry me directly only to universal good, thereby teaching me that I ought to make thee the only direct and primary object of my love. My God, I will love as thou teachest me, the first and direct motion of love shall be towards thee, and whatever I love besides thee, I will love only in and for thee.

I thank thee also, my God, for that thou hast made it so necessary for me to love universal good. Thou, O God, art this universal good, and I ought to love thee with the very same love wherewith I love happiness itself. O that I were as necessarily inclined to love thee as I am to love happiness! I do not desire to be trusted with any liberty in the love of thee. But this, my God, I cannot hope for, till I shall see thee as thou art. O let me therefore love thee to the utmost capacity of a free creature. Thou, O God, hast set no bounds to my love of thee, O let not me set any. My God, I do not, I love thee with all my heart, soul, mind and strength. Lord thou knowest all things, thou knowest that I love thee.

Contemplation IV—Man Consider'd as an Irregular Lover

The Aspiration

To thee, O my God, belongs praise and adoration for endowing me with those excellent powers of understanding and love, but to me shame and confusion of face, for misapplying the one and not attending to the dictates of the other.

I blush, O my God, and am ashamed to think that my nature should stand so much inclined to irregular love, a thing so full of mischief and folly, but much more that I myself should bring myself into such a state of impotence and depravation. My heart sheweth me the great foulness and abominableness of sin, and yet I find myself over prone to commit it. So foolish am I and ignorant, and even as a beast before thee.

But I desire, O my God, to be yet more vile. I am not vile enough in my own eyes, though too much so in thine. Nor can I ever be vile enough in my opinion, for being so vile in my nature. Strike me then I beseech thee with a deep and with a lively sense of my own wretchedness, and make me as humble as I am wicked.

And since, through the infirmity of my flesh, I am so apt to err in the conduct and application of my love, O hold thou up my goings in thy paths, that my footsteps slip not. Make me always to attend to that divine light of thine within my breast, and let the victorious sweetness of thy grace outcharm all the relishes of sensible good. But above all, keep thy servant from presumptuous sins, lest they get the dominion over me. And let all these words of my mouth, and this whole meditation of my heart be always acceptable in thy sight, O Lord, my strength and my redeemer. AMEN.

A Prayer of Melchior Ritter

O God, in thee alone can our wearied spirits find full satisfaction and rest, and in thy love is the highest joy. Lord, if we have thee we have enough; and we are happy if thou wilt but give peace to our consciences, and make us know how gracious and merciful thou art. Preserve in our hearts that peace which passeth all understanding; and make us better and holier in time to come. Strengthen those of us who are in any sorrow or perplexity by the inward comfort of thy Holy Spirit, and bid us know that our light affliction, which is but for a moment, worketh for us a far more exceeding and eternal weight of glory. For there will come a time when thou wilt bring us to the place of perfect rest, where we shall behold thy face in righteousness and be satisfied from thy eternal fulness. AMEN.